DIRTBIRDS'
SELF·HELP GUIDE
How to Have Confidence When You Feel Lower than a Snake's Arse

Sinead Culbert and Sue Collins are Dirtbirds, a comedy duo and social-media sensation, whose weekly Facebook sketches have led to a massive following and sellout tours throughout Ireland.

Sinead Culbert lives in Lusk, North County Dublin with her Dutch husband, who claims when he saw her it was love at first sight – or as he pronounces it, 'love at first shite'. Sinead has two children, Sophia and Leon, and her hobbies include panicking and finding ways to avoid doing housework.

Sue Collins lives in Dublin 8 with her husband, four children and Paddy the dog. Sue does have not have *any* hobbies *because* she has four children and Paddy the dog. When Sue isn't working she spends all of her time making large pots of spaghetti Bolognese and driving her children around to extra curricular activities that they don't want to do. She clocks an average of 10,000 kilometres per week.

DIRTBIRDS'
SELF·HELP GUIDE

How to Have Confidence When You Feel Lower than a Snake's Arse

SUE COLLINS &
SINEAD CULBERT

Illustrated by Ciara Kenny

First published in Ireland in 2019 by
HACHETTE BOOKS IRELAND

1

Cataloguing in Publication Data is available from the British Library

ISBN 978 1 5293 2565 2

Typeset in Adonis by redrattledesign.com

Printed and bound in Great Britain by Clays Ltd, Elcograf S.p.A

Hachette Books Ireland policy is to use papers that are natural, renewable and recyclable products and made from wood grown in sustainable forests. The logging and manufacturing processes are expected to conform to the environmental regulations of the country of origin.

Hachette Books Ireland
8 Castlecourt Centre
Castleknock
Dublin 15, Ireland

A division of Hachette UK Ltd
Carmelite House, 50 Victoria Embankment, EC4Y 0DZ

www.hachettebooksireland.ie

Dedicated to all the women of Ireland
who are hanging by a thread.

CONTENTS

Rising Above The Crap
– The New You

WHY WE WROTE THIS BOOK

We live in a world where women are expected to have the patience of Mother Teresa, the arse of Jennifer Lopez, the culinary skills of Nigella Lawson and the BMI of Elle Macpherson.

The pressure to be perfect is relentless. We've all seen that Insta pic of the 'perfect family' on the 'perfect holiday' with the nauseating hashtags – #feelingblessed #mylifeisamazing, i.e. #yourlifeisaloadofbollox.

In reality, that 'perfect family' probably fought for the entire two weeks of that 'perfect holiday' and, although they'd like you to believe they were in the Bahamas, they were probably only in Bray.

This book is a guide to help you navigate the barrage of bullshit that we are subjected to on a daily basis and remind you that there is no such thing as perfect ... except maybe Jamie Dornan's arse in *Fifty Shades Darker*.

WHY THIS IS THE SELF-HELP BOOK FOR YOU

If you ask yourself any of the following questions then this book is for you.

- ☞ Will mindfulness stop me from committing manslaughter when someone takes my space in the car park at Lidl?

- ☞ How do I stop myself from punching the guy from Airtricity at my front door?

- ☞ What do I do when stress has totally wrecked my face?

- ☞ When the kids are doing my head in, how do I stop myself from selling them on DoneDeal?

☞ How do I manage my stress levels when I see a garda checkpoint and my tax expired 8 months ago?

HOW TO USE THIS BOOK?

Regularly.

We recommend that you buy at least 25 copies of this book and put them in the following places:

☞ on your bedside locker

☞ in your handbag

☞ on your desk in the office (maybe hidden behind a plant)

☞ on the island in your kitchen

☞ on top of the washing machine

☞ on the dashboard of your car

☞ in your gym bag

☞ in the fridge

☞ in the shower

This book is best read while drinking a large glass of Sauvignon Blanc and eating a packet of Doritos (chilli flavour). We recommend that you pick it up frequently and, more importantly, put it down frequently.

This book can be used as a tool to give you new confidence, inner strength and greater self-esteem … it can also be used to shove under the leg of your broken coffee table to keep it steady.

Mindfulness (Better than Manslaughter)

One of the principles of mindfulness is trying not to react when you feel like slapping someone around the head because they're acting like a complete tool. As part of the practice, we are advised to take a few deep, mindful breaths and let the rage pass rather than smashing someone's windscreen with a hurley stick at the traffic lights because they cut across you. This is particularly useful to remember when you are standing at the self service check-out in Tesco.

HOW TO BE ZEN AT THE SELF-SERVICE CHECKOUT IN TESCO

The self-service checkout was originally designed to save us time when we are under pressure. However, even the Dalai Lama would struggle not to react to the following scenarios:

☞ When the customer in front of you is taking *three hours* to find the barcode on a loaf of bread.

☞ When there are six machines and only two are working (and the person with the bread is at one of them).

☞ When the machine tells you there's an 'unexpected item in the bagging area' and it turns out to be your child.

☞ When you call the assistant over and she has to punch in 500 different codes and use 300 different keys to try and fix the fecking thing.

☞ When the people in the 'normal queues' were served three hours ago and you're *still* trying to scan a packet of Hobnobs.

According to mindfulness practice, in these stressful situations we should breathe slowly and 'follow our breath' ... or else we may find ourselves following the assistant (with the big bunch of keys) down the confectionery aisle and hitting her around the head with a multi-pack of Tayto crisps.

HOW TO PRACTICE MINDFULNESS WHEN YOU ARE DRIVING BEHIND A FECKIN EEJIT

When you are on the M50 you may be find yourself driving behind someone who is doing under five kilometres an hour in the fast lane with their indicator on. This scenario can cause the following reactions:

☞ confusion as to what the eejit is doing

☞ frustration because you are unable to overtake the eejit

☞ a very strong desire to kill the eejit.

It can also trigger some of the following behaviours:

☞ screaming at the windscreen

☞ cursing like a trooper

☞ gnawing through your own seatbelt.

Practising mindfulness will stop you from doing the following:

☞ driving past him and giving him the fingers

☞ driving past him and mouthing obscenities

☞ driving past him, doing *all* of the above and then realising he is about 180 years old.

PRACTISING FORGIVENESS IN THE LIDL CAR PARK

Practising forgiveness is part of mindfulness, although, at times, this can be very difficult – especially when you are in a Lidl car park and an aggressive driver pulls into a parking space that you have been waiting on for over *ten minutes.*

In this situation, it is essential not to react, but to send them love and kindness. Do *not* do the following:

☞ park directly behind them so they can't get out

☞ key the side of their car as soon as they have gone into Lidl

☞ follow them in and ram them with your trolley.

PRACTISING PATIENCE AT THE ATM

Practising patience and tolerance can come in handy in many everyday situations. A good example of this is when you go to withdraw money from the ATM and the following things happen:

☞ The person in front of you tries to withdraw money using 200 different bank cards.

☞ You queue behind 20 people and by the time it's your turn it's out of service.

☞ You eventually find an ATM that works, put your card in and it says, 'insufficient funds'.

The Buddhists recommend doing a ten-minute meditation before going near an ATM or, failing that, withdraw all of your money from the bank and hide it under your mattress.

SCENARIOS WHICH REQUIRE A SHITLOAD OF DEEP BREATHING

☞ When you ring the tax office about your P45 and they leave you on hold for *that long* that by the time they answer, you need to enquire about your pension.

☞ When you're in the cinema watching *Toy Story 4* with your kids and you're crying – not because it's sad but because the little bastard behind you keeps kicking the back of your seat.

☞ When you're trying to book something online, but you can't read the security number on the back of your card and you've only got three seconds remaining.

☞ When you've asked your child if she needs to go to the toilet before a long journey and she says no, then changes her mind *just* as you get onto the M50.

FITNESS TIPS FOR WOMEN WHO CAN'T BE ARSED

In a recent study on attitudes to exercise, 60 per cent of Irish women said they would rather *eat their own arms* than go to the gym. Top excuses used by these women include:

☞ the dog ate my runners

☞ *Strictly Come Dancing* is on

☞ I couldn't be arsed today ... I swear to God I'll start tomorrow.

MOTIVATIONAL TIPS

☞ Hire a very attractive personal trainer, it'll motivate you to get up at the crack of dawn – to plaster on your foundation before he arrives.

☞ Record your activity on your Fitbit. When you see that you have done 10,000 steps in a day, you will feel really motivated (even if 5,000 of those steps are achieved by going over and back to the chipper).

☞ Arrange to exercise with a friend; by the time you've bitched about everyone you know, you'll have done ten kilometres without noticing.

Case Study

Fiona Lush from Dublin talks about her fitness levels

They've gone through the roof. I can now do three kilometres in under ten minutes.

I discovered this at ten to ten last Tuesday

night when I had run out of white wine and
realised the off-licence closed at ten. I never ran
as fast in my life. It's all about the motivation.

MYTHS ABOUT EXERCISING

Myth: Leaving your runners beside your bed will
motivate you to get up at 6 a.m. and go for a run.
Truth: You will forget that you have left them there, trip
over them and sprain your ankle (giving you the perfect
excuse not to have to exercise for the next six months).

Myth: If you don't feel like exercising, trick yourself by
telling yourself you're only going to do a five-minute
jog and then you'll end up running for ten kilometres.
Truth: After three minutes of desperately trying to
exercise, you'll go home and have a large piece of
chocolate cake.

Myth: If you put your tracksuit on first thing in the
morning you are more likely to go for a run.
Truth: No, you'll probably drop your kids to school,
bump into a friend, have a coffee with her and then
pretend to everyone that you went for a run.

Myth: Walking the dog is great exercise.

Truth: Walking the dog is not *real* exercise. You will have to stop at every second tree so she can have a piss and the *only* time you will break a sweat is when she does a massive poo and you realise you've forgotten the poo bags.

Myth: You look cool when you're running.

Truth: No, you don't. You look like Forrest Gump.

Myth: If you do yoga for an hour a day you will have a body like Jennifer Aniston.

Truth: No, you won't. Jennifer Anniston does yoga for 20 hours a day with a world-famous yogi and even sleeps in the downward dog position. You haven't a hope!

Myth: You will feel motivated by seeing how many calories you are burning on your Fitbit.

Truth: You will actually feel totally *deflated* because you'll realise that despite killing yourself jogging around the park seven times, you have only burned 200 calories, which is the equivalent of *one* chocolate biscuit (and you had two packets before you left the house).

Myth: Joining a fancy gym will make you exercise more.
Truth: Even if George Clooney was working at reception and Brad Pitt was handing out the towels, you *still* wouldn't get your lazy arse over to it.

THE IMPORTANCE OF TALKING SHITE TO OTHER WOMEN

It has now been scientifically proven that if a woman does not talk shite to another female for at least one and a half hours a day, she will implode. It is a well-known fact that women are actually better at talking than breathing.

Symptoms of *not* getting to chat to another woman for long periods of time include foaming at the mouth, howling at the moon and even resorting to sharing her 'feelings' with her husband.

THE NEED TO RABBIT ON FOR HOURS ON THE PHONE

Men are often – understandably – bewildered by a woman's

biological need to rabbit on to her friends for hours at a time. A woman can call a friend *to arrange to meet* for a chat (this call itself can last over three hours), she can then chat to the same friend on the phone *on the way* to meet her and *still* have plenty to talk about when she actually gets there.

The average time a man spends on the phone is about ten seconds ... except when his wife rings him.

TALKING ABOUT OUR PROBLEMS UNTIL WE LITERALLY CAN'T TALK ANYMORE

Studies have shown that when a woman is upset about something, she usually follows a particular pattern of behaviour. Firstly, she will call a female friend and discuss her problem in *great detail*. This will include *what* was said, *who* said it, *how* it was said, *why* it was said, *the expression on the face* of the person who said it and *how she felt* when it was said to her.

After this phone call, she will proceed to call every woman she can think of, including her sister, her mother, and her best friend in Australia, and have the exact same conversation with all of them.

Each one of these women will show great empathy to their friend, saying things like, 'Oh you poor thing', 'I know exactly how you feel' and 'You were absolutely right to do what you did' (even when they don't believe she was).

COUNSELLING SESSIONS IN THE TOILET OF A NIGHTCLUB

Women often strike up conversations with complete strangers while applying make-up in the toilets of a nightclub. These conversations can start by admiring the shade of the other woman's lipstick and quickly develop into an extremely personal discussion on the benefits of using the coil.

These therapy sessions in the toilets can last anything from five to twenty minutes, involve the input from other passing strangers and cover any topic, from the causes of a rosacea flare-up to the row you've just had with your husband.

A woman can enter the toilets just to apply her lip gloss and leave having saved someone's marriage.

Case Study

JUNE O'REILLY, NIAMH FORDE and STEPHANIE FLANAGAN are best friends who meet every Saturday for lunch. They have recently been entered into the Guinness Book of Records *for the most talking done at a lunch. Niamh explains how it happened*

We arrived at Gibney's hotel on Saturday, 12th April at 1 p.m. We started talking immediately because we hadn't see each other in a while — well, for two days.

It felt like we were only talking for a couple of hours, but then we noticed the hotel had been completely redecorated and the weather was much warmer outside. Stephanie looked at her phone and that's when we realised it was actually May 31st.

INSPIRATIONAL QUOTATIONS FROM REAL IRISH WOMEN

Life is hard. If it wasn't for the Valium, I'd be on drugs.

JOAN, LEGWEE, COUNTY CAVAN

When Marriage Melts Your Head

According to recent medical research, marriage triggers the release of *exactly* the same level of stress hormones as living in the wilderness with Bear Grylls, wrestling crocodiles, fighting off poisonous snakes and scaling 3,000-foot cliffs without safety gear.

According to the LSMPII (the Long-Suffering Married People of Ireland Institute), the biggest threat to a marriage is not extramarital affairs or even financial stress but actually the annoying things we do to each other on a daily basis.

These are just some of the extremely annoying behaviours that can devastate even the strongest marriage:

☞ Secretly turning down the heat on the hob when your partner is making the dinner.

☞ Claiming your partner's house keys are yours (even though you know damn well you lost your set in the pub last Friday night).

☞ Buying yet another NutriBullet from Aldi to add to the 200 you already have in the garage.

☞ Repeatedly losing your partner's mobile phone charger.

☞ Not putting the lid back on the raspberry jam properly.

☞ Snoring like a pig being run over by a freight train.

☞ Sweeping the floor and not bothering your arse to pick up the pile of dirt (leaving it for the kids, their friends and the dog to drag all over the house).

☞ Standing over your partner's shoulder and telling them how to cook pasta.

☞ Sneakily pulling the duvet over to your side of the bed and pretending you must have done it in your sleep.

THE CURSE OF CONSTANTLY COMPROMISING

According to Professor Laura Wornout from the Institute of There's No Point in Arguing, 'Nobody ever explains to us just how much compromise is required to make a marriage work. Marriage is basically doing stuff you don't want to do – all the jaysus time.'

In her new book *The Shit We Have To Do To Keep The Peace*, she highlights some of the things that you will find yourself doing in order to hold on to your marriage:

☞ Watching *Fastest Car* on Netflix and pretending to give a shit about whether the Lamborghini is faster than the Ferrari 488.

☞ Not commenting when your partner cooks the chicken at 200 degrees (even though you know he is going to burn the arse off it).

☞ Pretending the chicken he made tastes *amazing*, even though you've lost two teeth eating it.

☞ Trying not to cry your eyes out when he tells you that his parents are coming to stay for *three whole fecking weeks.*

☞ Trying not to kill your mother-in-law during those three fecking weeks.

THE DANGERS OF TOO MUCH COMPROMISE

Case Study

ELAINE SUFFER from County Leitrim, who has been married to Joe for seventeen years, discusses the dangers of compromising too much in a marriage

The other day I rang my husband to ask him what he wanted for the dinner. He said he was 'easy' ... but then went on to say that he didn't want beef, chicken, curry or pasta.

Finally, he said he wanted pork chops. I don't like pork chops but I agreed to it anyway – and that's when the resentment kicked in.

I bought them with great resentment, I cooked them with great resentment and then

I watched as he gnawed on the bone like some sort of wild dog.

It was at that point that I began fantasising about picking up the fork and stabbing him in the forearm.

Suddenly, he threw down the bone and said, 'Elaine, that was delicious.' I thought, *Oh my God, he does love me after all*, but then he said, 'You know what? A bit of apple sauce would have really made it.'

Anyway, the consultant said that he'll get feeling back in his arm in the next six months.

LIES WE TELL TO SAVE OUR MARRIAGE

Lie: I bought my shoes in a 70 per cent discount sale in Marks & Spencer.

Truth: They were new arrivals in Brown Thomas and they cost almost as much as our house.

Lie: I don't know *how* that scrape got onto to the side of the car.

Truth: You were trying to park while texting and rammed into a bollard ... there is even CCTV footage to prove it.

Lie: The weekend away in Amsterdam with the girls was quite *tame*, actually.

Truth: You drank for 72 hours straight, went to 23 different nightclubs, stole a tuk-tuk and got arrested for doing 45 kilometres around Leidseplein Square at 5 a.m.

Lie: Your Thai red curry is delicious, darling.

Truth: My head feels like it's on fire, I'm going to pass out, call an ambulance!

CRAP ADVICE THAT DOESN'T WORK

Date nights bring you closer

No, they don't. By the time you've booked the restaurant, had a row about the fact that you both forgot to book the babysitter, pleaded with the babysitter to come at short notice, found something decent to wear, had *another* row on the way to the restaurant, you are too wrecked to even talk to each other.

Doing adventurous things together is very romantic

No, it isn't. Seeing your partner jump out of a plane at 12,000 feet, flail around screaming in terror as he tries to open his

parachute with his face flapping around in the wind, is far from romantic and may prompt you to question your choice of spouse and file for divorce.

Taking up a hobby together will make you stronger as a couple

Not a chance. You take up badminton together and, by week three, your partner has become *so* competitive that all you want to do is hit him over the head with the racket and shove the shuttlecock where the sun don't shine.

WHEN COUPLE COUNSELLING GOES WRONG

Case Study

Sandra Stale from Longford, who has been married to Pat for 25 years, discusses her experience of marriage counselling

Myself and Pat, like most other couples, would often go through little bad patches, they'd only last for maybe three or four ... years, and then we'd be right as rain again.

One time we went through a *really* bad patch (which lasted ten years) and our friend suggested couple counselling.

In our first session, the marriage counsellor told us not to bother having sex for a while, which wasn't a problem for us because we hadn't even *spoken* to each other in five years.

She said to go home, get some massage oil and give each other a massage.

So, later, I started massaging Pat's feet and I don't know which toe I was rubbing but it was obviously connected to the bowels because he jumped up and ran towards the toilet.

However, he slipped on the tiles, flew into the air and landed on his back. He was in hospital for six weeks getting a hip replacement, God love him. It was awful for him, but the peace and quiet, and the time apart, really saved our marriage.

DIRTBIRDS' SELF-HELP GUIDE

HOW TO COPE WHEN YOUR HUSBAND GETS THE 'MAN FLU'

When a woman gets the flu she does the following:

- ☞ takes two paracetamol and drags her arse out of the bed

- ☞ doesn't complain ... because no one gives a shite anyway.

A recent study has shown that even if a woman is lying on the kitchen floor unconscious, a child will still stand over her and ask her what's for dinner.

When a man develops *the same flu*, he does the following:

- ☞ falls to his knees, shaking and shivering

- ☞ crawls into his bed like a wounded animal

- ☞ gasps for breath as if he's suddenly contracted the black plague

- ☞ whines, groans and even begs his wife to call an ambulance.

Final tip: Call the ambulance ... and let *them* tell the fecker there's nothing wrong with him.

A SURVIVOR'S GUIDE TO ANNOYING NEIGHBOURS

When we buy a house, we are concerned about location, proximity to schools, local transport and, of course, the all-important 'potential' to extend. However, what we *should* be concerned about is what kind of *lunatics* we will be living beside and the impact they may have on our mental health.

In 2018, a survey revealed that 80 per cent of people *can't stand the sight* of their neighbours, 90 per cent have fantasised about *killing* their neighbour and 75 per cent said that they would *rather live on the side of a mountain* in a remote village in Guatemala than continue living beside their current neighbours.

In this chapter we will discuss the different kinds of annoying neighbours and help you to identify the particular type of arsehole you are living next to.

THE NOSEY NEIGHBOUR

If you are unfortunate enough to live beside this kind of neighbour, you will not need Phonewatch or CCTV cameras as this nosey bastard will be watching you 24/7.

They will be able to tell you about *anyone* who goes in, comes out, passes by or even glances momentarily at your property. Their hobbies include clipping their front hedge so they can see everything and bombarding their neighbours with intrusive questions like:

> ☞ 'I see you round a lot more during the day. Have you lost your job?'

> ☞ 'I noticed there aren't as many men's clothes hanging on your washing line. Has your husband left you?'

> ☞ 'There was an official-looking man with a clipboard looking in your window on Wednesday at about 2 p.m. Did you not pay your TV licence?'

☞ 'I saw you chatting to the guy from Airtricity for 23 minutes and 48 seconds yesterday. Have you decided to change provider?'

THE PETTY NEIGHBOUR

These people are highly territorial and get their knickers in a *complete twist* over the most trivial things, like how many inches their neighbour's apple tree is hanging over their fence. They usually get themselves into positions of power, becoming the chairperson of the residents' association and get kicks from regularly objecting to any new development in the area (despite the fact that they haven't a clue what most of them are).

Their hobbies include placing traffic cones outside their house to protect their parking space (even though they don't own a car), visiting the local county-council offices to study their neighbour's plans for extending and strimming the weeds from the pavement ... but only on their side.

THE COMPETITIVE NEIGHBOUR

The neighbour that will cause your cholesterol to spike and your arteries to harden the most is the highly competitive neighbour. Her sole purpose in life is to ensure *her* house is the most *fabulous* on the road and constantly reminding you that yours looks a bit shit.

She extends her house every six weeks, gets a new kitchen every two years and adds a new breed of exotic fish to the enormous pond in her Japanese-style garden every other summer.

She regularly invites her neighbours around for coffee (not because she is friendly but because she wants to show off her 20,000 euro pure marble counter-top which was especially imported from Morocco).

If any of her neighbours get work done to their houses, it sends her into a complete frenzy and results in her doing the following:

☞ Hanging out of her back window to try and see inside the next-door neighbour's new extension.

☞ Hiding behind her lotus flower with binoculars to catch a glimpse of the colour of the new kitchen across the road.

☞ Jumping up and down on her children's trampoline to get a look at the new light fixtures in the house two doors down.

THE UNFRIENDLY NEIGHBOUR

In every neighbourhood, there is always one house with *all* of the blinds pulled down *all* of the time.

Even in an intense heatwave these people refuse to pull back their curtains or open their windows for fear someone might look in. Some may call them aloof or extremely private but the simple truth is ... they are just *unfriendly b******s.*

Inspirational Quotations from Real Irish Women

Visualisation really works. I visualised a tall, dark, handsome man staring into my eyes on my wedding day and it came true ... the priest was a complete ride.

NOREEN MURPHY, BASTARDSTOWN, WEXFORD

How Not To Look Like a Bag of Shite on Your Wedding Day

Tip 1: Buy a wedding magazine and pick a model with a look you would like to go for on your big day. But be realistic — there is only so much a beautician can do. Remember, she is a make-up artist, not a miracle-worker.

Tip 2: Most beauty experts will recommend going for a *natural* look for your wedding day. But remember, you weren't very 'natural looking' the night you met your fella, in fact he's probably never actually seen the *real* colour of your skin. So we recommend that if you want him to go through with the wedding ... *plaster it on.*

Tip 3: Stay away from low coverage foundation. Use high, high, high, high, high coverage foundation and apply at least 25–30 layers.

Tip 4: It's very important to use the right make-up brush when applying foundation. We recommend a paint brush – it is cheap, has very strong bristles and can do half your face in one stroke.

Tip 5: Apply shitloads of blusher to your cheeks as the blood will drain from your face every time you think of the 50,000 euro loan you took out of the credit union for your big day.

Tip 6: Use contouring and highlighting to create the illusion that you actually *have* cheekbones and hide the potato-face syndrome that most Irish women suffer from.

Tip 7: Always use waterproof mascara as you will get very emotional walking up the aisle. Not because you're so happy but because you've realised you're marrying the wrong man and you should be marrying his brother.

Tip 8: Don't shy away from lip fillers – the bigger the better. This way you can achieve the 'Angelina Jolie, bee-stung, I have just had my face kicked in' look.

Tip 9: HD eyebrows would look great on your wedding day but they are very expensive. If you don't have the cash and you want permanent eyebrows ... just use permanent marker (six for a euro in Dealz).

Tip 10: Do not wear a pair of false eyelashes ... wear three. This will create a 'doe-eyed, innocent look' giving the impression that you have only *ever* been with one man in your whole life ... even though you've probably slept with half the town.

Tip 11: If you make a complete balls of your make-up, don't lose your head. Cover it. Pull the veil right down over your face and keep it there for the whole day and no one will be any the wiser. (This might make drinking alcohol a little tricky. We suggest using a long straw.)

Tip 12: Don't wear control pants. They just push the fat somewhere else. The last thing you want in your wedding photos is to have all your stomach fat pushed up around your neck.

Tip 13: Confiscate all phones from your wedding guests as the last thing you want is for someone to post a photo of you on Instagram at 2 a.m. with your wedding dress tucked into your knickers playing air guitar to Guns N' Roses' 'Sweet Child of Mine'.

Tip 14: Choosing your bridesmaids is a very important decision. Don't get distracted by superficial things like friendship or loyalty. Focus on what's important ... like whether or not they are better-looking than you, slimmer than you or more photogenic. Remember, this is *your* day and it's *all about you.*

Tip 15: Do not use gradual fake tan. You run the risk of walking up the aisle with skin as pale as Nicole Kidman's and, sitting at the top table two hours later, looking like Donatella Versace.

Tip 16: A final tip for removing your make-up on your wedding night ... don't bother your arse.

THE ORDEAL OF ONLINE DATING

Gone are the days of the slow set where you could meet your future husband or wife to the soundtrack of 'Lady in Red' by Chris de Burgh. Real-time dating is a thing of the past (and so is Kajagoogoo) so let's embrace virtual romance.

The following tips will help you navigate online dating:

☞ If a guy's profile picture is of a golden retriever then he's probably not the 'sporty, good-looking guy' it claims he is.

☞ If his profile picture is a distant shot of him zip-lining across the Andes ... there is a reason it's a distant shot.

☞ Don't message each other for five years before you meet because there's a chance that when you do actually meet, you'll want to get away from him after five minutes.

☞ Always ring your date before you meet him. If he whispers when he answers, he is probably married or – worse – living with his mother.

☞ Meeting your date for a coffee can be safer ... but, be warned, it is *very* difficult to look calm and cool when you've had 125 Americanos.

☞ You *can* meet in a pub, but if you have to be carried out of the bar because you drank three pitchers of beer in under three minutes, you probably won't get a second date.

☞ If you're on a date and you realise you had more laughs meeting your bank manager to discuss your mortgage interest rate, excuse yourself and climb out the bathroom window.

How To Be Confident When You're Feeling Lower Than A Snake's Arse

Health and wellbeing is a multibillion-dollar industry with celebrities like Gwyneth Paltrow advising us to exist on a daily diet of one kale leaf, half an avocado and ten litres of filtered spring water from the Swiss Alps.

Gwyneth also encourages us to spend over 2,000 euro a month on products like lip balm made from the fat of a duck's arse or body lotion made of gold flakes and a crow's testicles.

So how do we develop real body confidence without having six personal chefs, five personal trainers and a team of make-up artists on call 24/7 to plaster on the slap?

SUE COLLINS & SINEAD CULBERT

Dee from Dundalk and Andrea from Ardee are beauticians, bloggers, vloggers, *boggers* and social influencers with a huge following ... in Dunleer.

Here they give real advice and practical tips on how the normal, average, exhausted Irish woman can feel good about her body again.

(Disclaimer: Dee and Andrea have never *actually* worked as beauticians nor done *any* professional modelling, in fact the *only* photograph ever published of them was in the social section of *The Fingal Leader* in 2005.)

TIPS FROM DEE AND ANDREA

To build up a positive relationship with your body, we recommend starting every morning by saying three affirmations to yourself in the mirror. Examples of affirmations regularly used include:

1. I am beautiful.

2. I am stunning.

3. I am very sexy.

However, we suggest that you should be *more realistic*. There is no point in lying to yourself. So here are more truthful affirmations that will probably resonate a lot better with you:

1. I am beautiful ... on the inside.

2. There is nothing wrong with me.

3. I am a harmless auld crathur.

If you repeat these affirmations at regular intervals throughout the day your confidence will soar.

HOW TO LOVE YOUR BODY WHEN NO ONE ELSE DOES

Step 1: Stand in front of a full-length mirror totally naked.

Step 2: Take a deep breath, stretch your right arm above your head ... and take the light bulb out. (Because no one wants to see *that* image in full light.)

Step 3: If you *do* see your naked body in full light ... take three Xanax.

Step 4: Slowly walk backwards, away from the mirror.

Step 5: Squint your eyes as much as you can.

Step 6: Look at yourself through the tiny slits of your eyes and say the following:

'It is what it is.'

Step 7: Have a glass of wine; you can't have good self-esteem without alcohol.

Remember: The more you drink, the better you look. Note: If you don't drink ... *start*.

THE SWANXSUIT: A SWIMSUIT WITH AS MUCH CONTROL AS 150 PAIRS OF SPANX

The following are some of the advantages and disadvantages of this ridiculously tight swimsuit:

Advantage: It will make you look three sizes smaller.

Disadvantage: You might break three ribs getting into it.

Advantage: Your waist will be tiny.

Disadvantage: Your face will be *blue* (from a lack of oxygen).

SUE COLLINS & SINEAD CULBERT

Advantage: Men will fall over themselves to talk to you.

Disadvantage: You could fall into a medical coma if you leave the suit on for too long.

HEALTH WARNINGS FOR THE SUPER SWANXSUIT

☞ You cannot swim in it (because you cannot breathe in it).

☞ You cannot walk in it (because you'll have *no* feeling from the waist down).

☞ You *can* lie down in it (but you can't get back up in it, so always bring a friend to the beach).

THE STRESS OF THE HOLY COMMUNION

REASONS WHY YOUR CHILD IS MAKING HER HOLY COMMUNION

- ☞ Your mother-in-law will disown you if she doesn't.

- ☞ Everyone else is doing it.

- ☞ You want everyone to see your new kitchen.

- ☞ It's a good excuse for adults to get drunk and jump up and down on a bouncy castle.

THINGS YOU NEED FOR THE BIG DAY

☞ An enormous bouncy castle in the shape of a unicorn.

☞ The number of an overpriced catering company.

☞ New outfits for everyone in the family, including the dog.

☞ A six-tiered butter cream custom-made First Holy Communion cake featuring lace, pearls, sugar rosary beads, ten marzipan doves, a giant pink bow and a six-foot glitter cross on the top.

☞ An offshore bank account for your child's Holy Communion money

☞ A spray tan for your eight-year-old to make her look like she's from Bali even though she's from Ballymun.

☞ A Holy Communion dress with a train so long that you have to hire a security guard to watch her on the bouncy castle in case she strangles herself.

☞ A helicopter to bring you to the local church even though there'll be nowhere to land it except on top of the nearby Supervalu.

☞ Two thousand bottles of prosecco.

USEFUL TIPS FOR MOTHERS ON THE BIG DAY

☞ Bring tissues because you *will* get very emotional at the ceremony. Not because your child is receiving the holy sacrament but because you spent over 2,000 euro on a dress she will *never* wear again.

☞ Apply fifty layers of concealer underneath your eyes to hide the large puffy black bags that have developed as a result of the ridiculous amount of organisation that has gone into this *one bloody day*.

☞ Wear sunglasses into the church, not to look cool, but to hide the fact that you have slipped into a coma while the other 8,000 children make their Holy Communion before your child does.

☞ Don't panic about your wobbly belly on the day. When the photos are being taken just grab the child with the biggest dress (even if it's not your child) and stick her in front of you. (If you're carrying *a lot* of weight you might need the *whole class.*)

☞ Look for special deals in hairdressers like 'mother and daughter up-styles with a free glass of prosecco'. You'll both have great hair and you'll be half cut heading down to the church.

☞ Practise doing what the Buddhists call the 'half smile'. This will not only make you look prettier but will also give the impression you are delighted to see your in-laws when you really can't stand the sight of them.

Case Study 1

KATY FAKE from Montenotte in Cork talks about her twin boys' Holy Communion

I wasn't surprised when Luan and Cuan were asked to do readings during the ceremony because they have *amazing* speaking voices and *incredible* charisma.

The day was going so well and they both looked *absolutely stunning* in their Ralph Lauren duck-egg-blue suits ... until the little feckers took them off in the church car park and changed into their Adidas tracksuits in front of EVERYONE. It was *absolutely humiliating.*

Case Study 2

SHARON CRASS from Dublin talks about the excitement of her daughter's Holy Communion

My daughter Shakira designed her *own* dress. It was inspired by the movie *Frozen*. It had Elsa on the front of it holding the baby Jesus and Olaf on the back with his tongue sticking out ready to receive the Holy Communion.

The food was ABSOLUTELY gorgeous ... then again, you can't beat Domino's pizzas. We had a great day, we all got completely hammered, there was even one fella who ended up twerking on the bar in his boxers – though, fair play to Fr Ryan, he really knows how to enjoy himself.

WHEN MAKING SCHOOL LUNCHES SENDS YOU OVER THE EDGE

Every year, 70 per cent of Irish households throw out approximately 1,000 uneaten cheese sandwiches, 600 half-eaten chicken wraps and 2,822 rotten squashed bananas from their children's lunchboxes.

Even the most health-conscious parents are having to scrape hummus and avocado dip off the bottom of their children's schoolbags and rescue carrot batons from inside their maths books.

According to the World Health Organization, leaking beakers and mouldy rolls are now officially considered a serious threat to the mental health of parents across the world.

Recently, online support groups have been set up to help parents cope with the stress of trying to come up with new ideas for the school lunches and advice is given on how not to kill their children when the *little feckers* don't eat it.

The following are some of the excuses children give for not eating their lunches:

☞ I didn't have enough time to eat. (Even though they've the *same amount* of fecking time to eat every day.)

☞ You give me yellow cheese and I only like red cheese. (You didn't even give them cheese *at all*.)

☞ My beaker spilled all over my spinach and tomato sandwich *by mistake*. (Yeah, right.)

☞ Maeve's mammy made hot paninis for everyone in the class so I wasn't hungry. (You *hate* Maeve's mammy.)

THE MYSTERY OF THE MISSING LUNCHBOXES

Every day, thousands of children go to school with nicely packed lunchboxes and come home without them. Despite intense searches of homes and schools, no one seems to be able to find the damn things.

This mystery has baffled millions of parents the world over and they are now resorting to using hidden cameras in schoolbags, as well as private investigators, GPS tracking devices and low-flying drones in a bid to locate the missing lunchboxes. The mystery still has not been solved.

DIVA DEMANDS FROM CHILDREN WHILE MAKING THE SCHOOL LUNCHES

As soon as you start making the school lunches, your sweet, angelic, timid little five-year-old will suddenly turn into Mariah Carey on speed. Firstly, she will start complaining bitterly about not wanting a ham sandwich, then she will refuse point blank to drink out of the pink beaker, scream hysterically at the suggestion of brown bread, and her head will spin like something from *The Exorcist* at the mere sight of an apple going into her lunchbox.

SOME OF THE MOST COMMON DEMANDS MADE OF PARENTS WHEN MAKING THE SCHOOL LUNCHES

☞ 'Take the strawberries out of the strawberry jam.'

☞ 'Don't give me the yogurt with the bits in it.'

☞ 'Don't give me the orange juice with the bits in it.'

☞ 'Cut the crusts off the bread.'

☞ 'Cut the bread into triangles.'

☞ 'Cut the triangles into smaller triangles.'

☞ 'Cut the smaller triangles into squares.'

Case Study

Extract from an interview with Carmel Glut, mother of four, from Limerick

Interviewer: Do you find it difficult to come up with new ideas for the school lunches?

Carmel: Oh yeah, I'm always trying to make them healthy lunches.

Interviewer: What do you give them?

Carmel: Just the usual, sandwiches, crisps, yogurt ... Red Bull.

Interviewer: Are they fussy?

Carmel: Yeah, I always have to cut the crusts off the sandwiches. It's a disaster.

Interviewer: Why?

Carmel: Because I always end up eating them ... I'm after putting on two stone this year from eating crusts alone.

THE HORROR OF HOMEWORK

Homework is a compulsory part of Irish education. It is considered by educators to be a positive way to reinforce what the child has learned during the day, but most mothers and fathers believe it is a stressful, unnecessary and complete bloody waste of time.

Reactions to having to do homework often include shouting, stamping of feet and hiding under the kitchen table ... and that's just the parents.

Five ways to stop yourself from having a nervous breakdown while helping with homework:

1. Never let your child see how intimidated you are by his Maths homework. Your child is not yet aware that you are absolutely bloody brutal at Maths and that you only got a D in Pass Maths even with *three years* of intensive grinds.

2. When you don't know the answer to a question like 'How many faces are on a cylinder?', just fake a smile, guess an answer and remind yourself that this information will be of *no use* to your child in her adult life. It will not help her in life-threatening situations and it will definitely not make for interesting dinner-party conversation.

3. Take a deep breath before you start doing any Irish homework with your child. Remind yourself that you did *Honours* Irish at school ... even if it was only for two days and then you were sent down to pass. Your Irish vocabulary may not be extensive but you do know some very useful phrases like *ar nós na gaoithe* (as fast as the wind), *Tá mo chroí i mo bhéal* (My heart is in my mouth) and *Tá an madra ag tafann* (The dog is barking).

4. Keep your phone charging beside you at *all times* because you will inevitably be googling *absolutely everything*.

5. When you *think* the homework has been completed your child may tell you that she is also required to build a European city out of recycled materials. Upon hearing this news, your body may start shaking uncontrollably and you might start to foam at the mouth. Try to calm yourself and please refrain from doing the following stupid things:

    ☞ sending a death threat to your child's teacher in the homework notebook

    ☞ downing a bottle of dry white in one go

    ☞ Paying your childminder to do the project for you.

Instead, just smile at your child, hand them some toilet roll fillers and wish them luck.

Case Study 1

The following is an interview with an ordinary woman, CAROL THICKE from Cavan

Interviewer: Do you find doing homework stressful in your house?

Carol: Yes, it's a bloody nightmare.

Interviewer: Why is that?

Carol: Because I really struggle helping my son Calvin with his homework and apparently it gets harder and harder every year.

Interviewer: And what year is your son in now?

Carol: Senior Infants.

Case Study 2

CARMEL FORTUNE from Finglas discusses how she helped her son when he was doing his Leaving Certificate

Interviewer: Did you try and help him study?

Carmel: No, I gave him plenty of space.

Interview: What did you do, keep out of his room and stay downstairs?
Carmel: No, I went to Majorca for three weeks.

WHEN THE KIDS WRECK YOUR HEAD DURING THE SUMMER

As the summer holidays approach an acute sense of panic spreads across the country as parents desperately try to figure out what in the name of jaysus they will do with the kids for two fecking months.

They start scouring the internet and school noticeboards searching manically for summer camps to stick their little darlings into. It doesn't matter what the summer camp actually is ... as long as it doesn't finish *before 4 p.m.*

Dr Summersolong from Tokyo has researched the negative impact on parents spending 24 hours a day with their children. Her research has shown that having no breaks from children can cause parents to lose the following:

☞ their ability to have an adult conversation

☞ their sense of humour

☞ their sense of time

☞ their pride in the way they look

☞ one of their children (if they go to a funfair)

☞ their will to live.

Case Study

RHONDA BLEARY-EYED from Blanchardstown talks about the struggle of keeping the kids entertained during the summer holidays

It costs a fortune during the summer taking the kids on day trips. I would easily spend about 40 euro a day – 20 on petrol, 10 on ice-creams and 10 on cans of Dutch Gold in Tesco on the way home ... 'cause you'd need a few drinks after having the kids all day.

PROFESSOR ENDA ME-TETHER GIVES SOME TIPS ON HOW TO COPE WITH THE KIDS DURING THE SUMMER

1. Get up at 4 a.m. and do three hours of meditation *before* the little f***ers get up.

2. Drink 18 strong cups of coffee first thing in the morning to keep you from slipping into a coma when you go to the *same pet farm* over and over again.

3. Encourage them to use their imagination – let them *imagine* you've taken them somewhere for the day.

4. Stick them in front of the TV if you start to feel your patience wane, it's better they watch *The Incredible Hulk* than watch *you* turn into the incredible hulk in real life.

5. Know your limits. Don't bring your kids' friends to the park with you, you'll only have to *pretend* you like them – and it's hard enough pretending you like your *own* kids.

CRAP IDEAS ONLINE FOR 'FUN, FREE ACTIVITIES'

If you look online, you'll find some ridiculous suggestions that will *apparently* entertain your children for hours at a time. The following is a breakdown of how much time these activities *actually* take.

Baking cookies with your kids

30 minutes trying to stop the kids from licking the spatula

20 minutes scraping the burned cookies off the tray

5 hours cleaning the fecking mess.

Go fly a kite

6 hours waiting for the wind to pick up

2 minutes *actually* flying the kite

3 hours detangling it from a tree.

Visiting a museum

2 minutes looking at paintings

35 minutes having a nervous breakdown because your children are knocking into priceless one-off sculptures.

Blowing bubbles

This will entertain your children for whole three-and-a-half minutes.

Fun Facts about the Morning Routine

DID YOU KNOW?

☞ Most parents burn about 300 calories every morning running up and down the stairs trying to get their kids up for school. (And then consume 6,000 calories comfort eating to get over the stress of it.)

☞ 75 per cent of parents get foot injuries from stepping on Lego while chasing their children around with a toothbrush.

☞ 95 per cent of parents smell their children's breath because they do not believe the little chancers have brushed their teeth.

☞ On average parents spend 25 minutes every morning desperately searching for a matching pair of socks.

☞ 96 per cent of kids end up going to school wearing odd socks.

☞ 85 per cent prefer Coco Pops to Bran Flakes.

☞ 100 per cent would prefer to eat their own arms than eat porridge.

☞ Dogs within a hundred-mile radius are frequently traumatised by the high-pitch screeching children make when they are getting their hair brushed.

☞ The average parent repeats the phrase 'Put your shoes on' over 200 times between 8.15 and 8.30 a.m.

☞ 72 per cent of parents spend ten minutes every morning looking for bicycle helmets and 25 minutes trying to persuade their kids to wear them.

☞ 67 per cent of parents find themselves filling in and signing forms (that should have been done the night before) *two minutes* before they leave the house.

☞ 50 per cent of parents leave their kids to school and have to come back home because their child has forgotten a ukulele, a lunchbox, Irish-dancing shoes, a hurley or a homework copy.

Are You Getting Enough 'Me Time'?

TAKE THE QUESTIONNAIRE

1. Has it been over ten years since you've finished a sentence without a child interrupting you?

2. Do you apply your make-up while driving to work at 120 kilometres an hour on the M50?

3. Has it been 800 years since your last facial?

4. Do you get very excited about going to SuperValu for milk just so you can flick through the magazines and fantasise about being on Heidi Klum's yacht?

5. Do you own a lipstick from 1998?

6. Do you sign up for shit you *don't want to do* just to get out of the house? (Like a 28-day Pilates challenge or becoming the chairperson of the residents' association.)

7. Do you cry a little when you pass a travel agency and see all the *amazing* holidays you'll *never* go on? (Especially the *adult-only* wine-tasting tour in Tuscany.)

8. Is your poor dog completely *over-walked* because taking him out is the only time you can hear yourself think?

9. When you look at yourself in the mirror do you tell yourself that the *huge black bags* underneath your eyes are just bad lighting in that particular room? (And then go into five other rooms and realise ... it's not the lighting.)

10. Do you jump at the chance to bring the broken Hoover back to DID Electrical just so you don't have to put the kids to bed?

11. Was *Titanic* the last film you saw with your husband in the cinema?

12. Do you own a library of self-care books but *never* get the time to actually read them?

13. Would you consider committing a serious crime because at least in prison you might get some alone time and your meals would be made for you?

If you answered Yes to over ten questions, you *badly* need to take a holiday ... for about a year.

Inspirational Quotations from Real Irish Women

Treat others the way you would like to be treated ... except Eleanor from the PTA, she's a *right* pain in the arse.

MAGGIE, DUBLIN 6

How To Be a Yummy Mummy

'Yummy mummy' is a relatively new term coined to describe mothers from middle-class areas who think they are *the dog's bollox*.

They spend their time:

☞ Running 800 marathons a year and posting 800 pics of each of them on Instagram.

☞ Doing all kinds of yoga classes, including yogalates, hot yoga, extremely hot yoga ... *burn the arse off ya* yoga.

☞ Organising charity coffee mornings with names like 'Meringues for Measles', 'Scones for Crones' and 'Eccles Cake for Erectile Dysfunction'.

The activity yummy mummies seem to enjoy *the most* is competing with each other on everything from the size of their extensions to how long they can stay in the downward dog position without passing out.

HOW TO LOOK LIKE A YUMMY MUMMY

☞ **Wear expensive exercise gear every morning:** This gives the impression that you are a superior being who has already done a 10K run before anyone else was awake.

☞ **Wear a full face of make-up at all times:** Including when you're jogging, at the gym, at yoga class and even when you're sitting in the jacuzzi.

☞ **Look fabulous collecting the kids from school:** Wear overpriced skinny jeans from Benetton, a gleaming white blazer (which means you can't have *any* physical contact with your child or he'll ruin it), sunglasses so big that your head looks the size of a peanut and a pair of Hunter Wellies (even in a heatwave).

☞ **Buy a ridiculously large SUV four-wheel drive vehicle:** Designed for off-road, rugged and mountainous areas, even though you live in a quiet, leafy suburb.

DirtBirds' Self-Help Guide

HOW TO BEHAVE LIKE A YUMMY MUMMY

☞ **Deny getting Botox and fillers:** Even though a six-month-old baby has more lines on its face than you do.

☞ **Project the image of a perfect family on Instagram:** Even though your marriage is hanging by a thread, your kids are spoilt little b******s and you are extremely close to a nervous breakdown.

☞ **Follow crap advice from yummy mummy bloggers:** Follow bloggers with names like Penny Plunkett O'Connor who give ridiculous parenting advice, like 'What to wear when you're bringing your small children to the doctor'.

☞ **Drink a skinny cappuccino from a keep cup and talk about your amazing new personal trainer called Carlos** (who is from Tallaght).

☞ **Walk around Brown Thomas for at least six hours a day pretending to shop:** Even though you can't afford it.

This coffee - AMAZING!

Yoga - AMAZING!

AMAZING!

UH-MAZING!

☞ **Follow a strict vegan diet:** Not because you want to save the planet, but because Victoria Beckham is doing it.

☞ **Send your children to an expensive private school:** Not because the teaching is better, but because someone famous sent their children there.

Case Study 1

Yummy mummies spend a lot of time watching their neighbours closely and competing with them on any home improvements they make.

A recent case of this took place in Blackrock, County Cork between neighbours EIMEAR BYRNE O'CASEY and ELEANOR O'CONNER SLATTERY in the summer of 2017.

The feud began when Eleanor got a large extension onto her kitchen. 'It was always my dream to extend my kitchen right out into the garden, out as far as possible, a kitchen that goes out, out, out.'

Eimear Byrne O'Casey watched the build closely and decided that she too wanted an extension but that hers needed to go 'out and up'.

When Eleanor realised that Eimear's extension would be bigger than hers, she immediately called her architect and insisted she wanted 'to build out, up and down'.

Against the advice of both her architect and

her husband, Eleanor went subterranean and built an underground swimming pool, gym and movie theatre.

In a jealous rage, Eimear ordered her team of builders to build her *another* three-storey extension to the *side* of her house with breathtaking views, a rooftop landscaped garden and a revolving cocktail bar.

Over a period of five years, the women continued to extend their houses in a bid to outdo each other – until both families were declared bankrupt.

Eimear had to abandon the build, which caused serious structural damage and led to the side of her house falling down. Her husband is filing for divorce and she now lives in her revolving cocktail bar alone.

Eleanor was forced to open her underground swimming pool to the public and now works in a local coffee shop. Her husband has left her for her architect ... John.

The court case with An Bord Pleanála is ongoing.

Case Study 2

Decorating the house and buying the latest appliances is a yummy mummy obsession.

SORCHA DOYLE O'SHEA spent over 700,000 euro on her kitchen, which boasts a marble countertop imported specially from Morocco, a smart refrigerator with a built-in video camera and a state-of-the-art, self-cleaning, triple NEFF oven

Interviewer: What do you love most about your new kitchen?

Sorcha: My smart kitchen is really a dream come true. But my favourite appliance is my 20-ring voice-activated gold-plated hob.

Interviewer: Wow, you must be doing a lot of cooking these days, Sorcha.

Sorcha: Em ... actually, no, we've been living on takeaway for the past few weeks.

Interviewer: Why is that?

Sorcha: Because we don't know how to switch the f***ing thing on!

Case Study 3

Yummy mummies send their children to a lot of extracurricular activities hoping that they will become sporting legends or musical geniuses – Sian talks about the need not to overdo it

I don't want to be one of those pushy parents, so I don't force my kids to do *too many* extra-curricular activities. My daughter Caoimhe only does swimming, piano and ballet ... on a Monday.

On a Tuesday she does dancing and drama, on a Wednesday she does gymnastics and cello, on a Thursday she does violin and art, on a Friday she does chess and on a Saturday she does sailing, wall-climbing and hill-walking.

Sunday is free ... except for choir and CoderDojo, which she does through Mandarin.

How To Manage Your Stress Levels When You See a Garda Checkpoint

The sight of a garda checkpoint has been reported to trigger acute anxiety in most Irish people. The following are some common reactions to seeing the blue flashing lights up ahead:

- ☞ Suddenly feeling like you have a dead body in the boot of your car and cocaine with a street value of two million euro.

- ☞ Praying to Jesus, Buddha and Allah that the guards won't notice your tax is out of date by six months.

☞ Cutting across a field and scaring the shite out of a load of sheep in an attempt to find another route.

☞ Imagining yourself being sent to prison and not seeing your children for ten years ... then thinking it mightn't be such a bad thing.

☞ Panicking about how long alcohol takes to leave your system ... even though you only had Baileys cheesecake the night before.

When you do eventually get to the top of the queue and the garda has no interest in your tax disc and explains that there has been an accident up ahead, you say the one thing you should never say when you hear this information: 'Oh thank God.'

WHAT YOU DO WHEN YOU GET THROUGH THE CHECKPOINT:

☞ Flash your lights manically at an oncoming car to warn them about the guards ... then realise the car you're flashing at *is* the guards.

☞ Feel so relieved they didn't notice your tax was out of date that you put your foot down, break a red light and get done for speeding.

☞ Ring your sister to warn her that the guards are there and get done for being on the phone while driving.

ARE YOU BATTLING WITH BURNOUT?

A recent study has revealed that 95 per cent of Irish adults are suffering from burnout and don't even know it. (Let's face it, they don't know ANYTHING, they're *that* burnt out. Women are particularly vulnerable to burnout because of the eight million jobs they have to do daily.

Below is a breakdown of what a typical Irish woman has to do in an average day:

☞ 30 minutes trying to get her children up and 30 minutes trying NOT to react to the grumpy little b******s.

☞ 4 hours driving her kids to extracurricular activities they really don't want to go to.

☞ 20 seconds putting on her make-up while driving on the M50.

☞ 2 hours repeatedly picking up Lego from the kitchen floor.

☞ 2 hours cooking a meal that the kids won't eat.

☞ 1 hour trying to psyche herself up to put the laundry away.

☞ 10 minutes depressing the bejaysus out of herself by looking at photos of Elle Macpherson's bikini body in *Hello!* magazine.

☞ 2 hours yelling at the kids to stop pulling the heads off each other.

☞ 15 minutes fantasising about selling her children on eBay.

☞ 5 hours sleeping before her husband wakes her up snoring like a fecking bear.

☞ 3 more hours staring menacingly at her husband, who is still snoring like a fecking bear.

BURNOUT QUESTIONNAIRE

1. Do you keep opening the fridge throughout the day staring longingly at the Pinot Grigio wishing it was after 5 p.m.?

2. Do you drink three bottles of Pinot Grigio as soon as it turns 5 p.m.?

3. Do you get into a lift, stand waiting for ten minutes, wonder why it isn't moving and then realise you haven't actually pressed the button?

4. Do you drive for 150 kilometres before you remember that you actually only intended to go to the local shop?

5. Do you cry at toilet-roll ads?

6. Do you go to important business meetings in your slippers?

7. When you see the words 'insufficient funds' at the ATM do you start crying uncontrollably in the middle of SuperValu?

8. Have you ever filled your car, driven off, noticed blue smoke coming out of the exhaust pipe and realised you've just filled your petrol car with diesel?

9. Have you ever pulled up at a petrol station, realised your fuel door is on the other side, driven around to another pump only to realise that your fuel door is *still* on the wrong side?

10. Have you ever driven off from a petrol station with the fuel door hanging open and a takeaway coffee on the roof of your car?

If you answered Yes to all of the above, you are *fried as f**k* and a danger to yourself and society at large.

ARE YOU THE PERFECT PARTNER OR A MASSIVE PAIN IN THE HOOP?

Your husband decides to grow huge sideburns and starts to resemble Wolverine.

Do you:

   a.   Tell him you are ok with the face of Wolverine as long as he promises he will have the body to go with it?

   b.   Tell him that you too will grow facial hair if he doesn't get rid of them?

   c.   Wait till he's asleep and shave them off?

It's your birthday and, instead of the bracelet you've been hinting at for the past six months, he buys you a cheap scented candle.

Do you:

a. Contemplate expressing disappointment but remind yourself that everyone gets it wrong sometimes and relationships are all about compromise?

b. Say nothing, wait for *his* birthday and buy him an air freshener for the car?

c. Pick up the candle, look at him lovingly, light it ... and throw it at him?

You go away for the weekend and, when you return, your husband has surprised you by painting the house 'slime green'.

Do you:

a. Say you *love* it, then run up the stairs and scream into your pillow for three hours?

b. Thank him profusely but then surprise *him* the next time *he* goes away by painting it white again?

c. Divorce him?

SUE COLLINS & SINEAD CULBERT

Your phone bill arrives and it's sky high. You know it's your fault because you were talking for seventeen consecutive hours to your best friend who lives in Canada.

Do you:

    a.   Admit that it is you who ran up the bill, but your friend needed to talk at length about something serious (even though you were only talking about the colour of her new kitchen counter tops)?

    b.   Say your phone has been stolen and that you've *no idea* who has been making three-hour calls to your mother?

    c.   Hide the bill and hope he doesn't notice the €2,000 euro coming out of the joint account?

Your husband is waiting for you to get ready for a dinner date: you are already late.

Do you:

    a.   Apologise profusely, then put your makeup on in the car and arrive looking like a drag queen?

b.   Tell him you're almost ready, even though you still have to put on your primer, foundation, highlighter, mascara, lipstick and straighten your hair?

c.   Put on the football and give him a can of beer? Hopefully he won't notice an hour going by.

Your partner says he's going for 'one' after work and arrives home plastered at 5 a.m.

Do you:

a.   Let him away with it – so you can do exactly the same thing next weekend when you go out with the girls?

b.   Make him sleep in the sitting room without a duvet, heating ... or the couch?

c.   Mess with his head the following morning and ask him if he really meant what he said to you last night (even though he said nothing because he was too plastered to speak)?

Your husband is boring the arse off everyone at a party with a 'funny story' he is telling.

Do you:

    a.   Jump on the table and start doing the floss to distract everyone?

    b.   Shout 'Fire!' and get everyone out of the kitchen so the humiliation will end?

    c.   On the way home, tell him that you love him but if he ever tells that story again you'll leave him?

It's Valentine's Day, you bought him a card and he gives you nothing in return.

Do you:

    a.   Hide the card you bought him, along with the deep resentment you now feel?

    b.   Tell him you forgive him for not getting you one – if he makes the dinner and puts the kids to bed for a week?

    c.   Reach for a hurley stick?

Mostly A: in his eyes you may be the Perfect Partner. (In reality you're probably sleeping with his best friend.)

Mostly B: Don't give it the couple counselling.

Mostly C: Your husband is probably filing for divorce as we speak.

Inspirational Quotations from Real Irish Women

I never cheat on my husband ... why would you have a burger when you've got a battered sausage at home?

SALLY KEANE, NOBBER, COUNTY MEATH

TEXT MESSAGES AT THE BEGINNING OF A RELATIONSHIP VERSUS TEXT MESSAGES TEN YEARS LATER

THE START OF A RELATIONSHIP	10 YEARS LATER
Good morning beautiful, last nite was amazing ... can't wait to see you again.	Get milk.
Hi, gorgeous , pick you up at 9 p.m. ... booked us into that great new restaurant on the seafront.	My mother's coming over for dinner.

Hi, sexy, you free Saturday? I was thinking maybe we could go to the movies, have a liquid lunch and maybe meet Brian and Sarah for drinks in The Q Hotel.	You'll HAVE to take Liam to his football match on Saturday 'cause I'm taking Sean to a birthday party and Mia to Irish dancing ... will pick up bottle of wine from Aldi if I have time.
You: Out with girls ... wish I was there with you. Him: I can collect you in ten minutes!	You: Out with the girls ... can't get a cab ... can you come pick me up? Him: Seriously ... it's 4 a.m., get the Nitelink.
Lying in my bed ... can still smell your perfume on my pillows.	Standing in the kitchen, can still smell the dog piss ... thought you cleaned it????

Making your favourite tonight ... sushi.	There's leftover bolognese in the fridge.
I'm wrecked today ... you were great last night.	I'm wrecked today ... you were snoring last night.

How To Look Ten Years Younger (or Maybe Just Not As Wrecked-Looking)

Beautician Dee from Dundalk (who never fully qualified as a beautician, having left the course after three days) and model Andrea from Ardee (who has never actually modelled in her life except for a fundraiser for the local GAA where no money was raised) run a beauty salon called Flip And Rip in Dundalk.

Below is their practical approach to looking younger

STOP GOING ON THE LASH

According to Jennifer Lopez, the secret to looking young is to give up drinking alcohol *completely*. This is excellent advice but we all know that Irish women would rather give up oxygen than give up the drink.

However, the liver does need a break, so we recommend giving up the drink from Monday right through until ... Tuesday morning, and then you can drink the head off yourself for the rest of the week.

SLEEP YOUR ARSE OFF

Melania Trump believes that getting enough sleep is what keeps her looking young. According to our sources, she gets 14–16 hours sleep a night. (Although it's safe to say that we'd probably *all* go to bed at 6 p.m. and pretend to be in a coma if Donald Trump was getting into the bed beside us.)

KEEP HYDRATED BUT *STAY AWAY FROM THE WATER*

Apparently, Cameron Diaz drinks two litres of water a minute. We do not recommend this as water is possibly *the most boring drink on the planet* ... no matter what you 'infuse' it with (unless it's vodka).

Instead, we recommend drinking two bottles of Lucozade a day – it's a tasty alternative, it's great for hangovers and it will give you a lovely orange glow.

DON'T GET RAVAGED BY THE RAYS

Irish skin generally comes in three shades: pink, purple and blue. This is very depressing, but it also means that we have to be super careful in the sun.

Irish people have been known to burn when they are sitting *inside* their houses, swimming underwater or standing on their balcony in the middle of the night. To avoid getting scalded to death, we recommend using factor 2,000 or ... fecking off to Iceland.

FORGET THE FRINGE

Apparently getting a fringe hides the wrinkles on your forehead and makes you look much younger, but unless you are *prepared to grow it down your chin* ... you're fooling no one.

TRY AND SMILE

Experts say optimists tend to look better as they age. Unfortunately, Irish people spend so much time whinging and whining about everything that they often look 800 years old when they're only 18.

Now you can't see ANY wrinkles!

STAY AWAY FROM SPECIAL OFFERS ON BOTOX

If you see a flashing neon sign outside a clinic saying, 'Botox in 25 areas for 25 euro with a free bottle of prosecco', *do not go in*. The chances are the beautician has had a bottle of prosecco herself, bought the Botox online for three euro and learned how to inject it from a YouTube video that morning.

ANTI-AGEING PRODUCTS RECOMMENDED BY DEE AND ANDREA

- ☞ 'Fucked For Time Foundation': Make-up for extremely busy women.

- ☞ 'My Face Is Sliding Down My Neck': A firming serum for exhausted women.

- ☞ 'My Lips Are Disappearing in Front of My Eyes': Lip plumper.

- ☞ 'Whinge-Proof Mascara': For the hormonal woman.

- ☞ 'Hide My Turkey Neck': tightening cream.

☞ 'What Just Happened to My Face': Rosacea cream.

☞ 'Jesus Look at My Jowls': Lifting cream.

☞ 'The Face Is Flaking off Me Foundation': Make-up for the woman with skin as rough as a badger's arse.

THE NEW 'WRINKLED AND WRECKED' RANGE OF PRODUCTS:

☞ 'How Did *That* Happen?': Hyaluronic hydro boost.

☞ 'The Morning-After': Face mask.

☞ 'No Point in Looking in the Mirror': Night cream.

☞ 'Desperate-Looking Décolletage': Day cream.

☞ 'Better Late Than Never': Body lotion.

☞ 'Hide My Hoods': Eye lift serum.

PARENTING IS A PAIN IN THE ARSE

There are many stressful jobs in the world, like being a CEO of a large company, a brain surgeon, a firefighter or a bomb disposal expert, but *none* will send you closer to a nervous breakdown than being a parent.

The market is saturated with parenting books giving totally unrealistic advice and leaving parents feeling confused, stressed and doing the one thing they don't want to do ... *turn into our own parents.*

MYTHS ABOUT PARENTING

Myth: Bribing your child is always a bad thing.

Truth: If ten euro gets the whole house cleaned ... you'd be mad not to.

Myth: You're a good parent if you never shout at your kids.

Truth: You're an absolute bloody *saint* if you never shout at your children – in fact, there's a good chance you're a robot.

Myth: Fighting in front of your kids will damage them.

Truth: Unless you are Angelina Jolie and have 800 nannies on standby ready to whisk your children away whenever you want to bite the head off your husband, this is completely impossible.

Myth: Never use the word 'no' with your children and they will become confident, self-reliant, well-adjusted adults.

Truth: Never use the word 'no' with your children and they will become spoiled, self-entitled little sociopaths who will be in prison before their tenth birthday.

Myth: Your children will bring you closer together.

Truth: No, they won't, the constant sleep deprivation, disagreements over Calpol dosage and the relentless

SUE COLLINS & SINEAD CULBERT

sibling fighting will kill *any* hope of romance returning ever, ever, ever again.

Myth: Good parents always enjoy their children.
Truth: Good parents always enjoy their children ... when they're asleep.

Myth: The 'terrible twos' is a difficult phase for a parent.
Truth: Every jaysus phase is difficult for a parent.

Below are some pearls of wisdom from normal, down-to-earth Irish women who are on the front line of parenting every day.

WHEN SIBLING FIGHTS ARE MORE VIOLENT THAN *GAME OF THRONES*

A recent study on siblings shows that the desire to beat each other into a pulp is part and parcel of their development. The following findings give an idea of the techniques and torture methods most commonly used:

☞ 15 per cent like to wrestle each other to the ground and punch the heads off each other.

☞ 30 per cent enjoy giving each other 'dead arms'.

☞ 15 per cent like to fart in each other's faces.

☞ 20 per cent elbow each other in the ribs until they hear a crack.

☞ 10 per cent delight in flicking each other with a rolled-up tea towel.

☞ 10 per cent use psychological techniques like hiding at the top of the stairs, jumping out and frightening the shite out of each other.

MANAGING THE MAYHEM

Many parents have devised their own techniques to cope with the trauma of sibling fighting. These include:

1. screaming at them

2. pleading with the guards to arrest them

3. sending them to the Gaeltacht (even when the Gaeltacht isn't open)

4. changing their name by deed poll and completely disowning them.

Case Study

EMMA WORNOUT from Cork talks about sibling fighting

Interviewer: What do you do when your children are fighting?

Emma: I just put my earphones in and let them sort it out themselves, that way they learn the skill of conflict resolution.

Interviewer: When was the last time you did this?

Emma: Yesterday. I heard them rowing and I stayed upstairs till it was over.

Interviewer: And did they resolve the conflict themselves?

Emma: Well ... after we came out of A&E. You see, Aoife had hit Ciarán across the face with an iPad.

Interviewer: So they were talking again?

Emma: Well, Aoife was talking but Ciarán couldn't 'cause he'd lost six teeth.

Making Breakfast for The First Child

Making Breakfast for The Third Child

A SIMPLE SOLUTION TO GETTING MORE SLEEP

Case Study 1

DEBORAH CHANCER, mother of two from Finglas, northwest Dublin works in the 24-hour Chinese takeaway Wok Around the Clock

Debs: We weren't getting any sleep at all 'cause my daughter Shakira was coming in to our room every night at about 4 a.m. She was afraid of monsters. And, let's face it, you can't throw a six-year-old out of your room 'cause they're afraid of monsters, it's too cruel, isn't it?

Interviewer: So what did you do?

Debs: Well, one night I had a great idea. I decided I would wait for her in my room ... *dressed up as a monster.* I scared the shite out of her and she hasn't been back since.

Case Study 2

CARMEL FORTUNE, from Cabra, works part-time in the local café, Angela's Rashers – she is a huge fan of the Kardashians and is a mother to six children: Kourtney, Kim, Khloe, Rob, Kendall and Kylie

I couldn't get pregnant for ages, we actually thought my fella was firing ... *caps.* We considered adopting a Chinese baby but the problem was ... neither of us can speak Chinese. We also thought about having the UVF treatment but someone told us you have to go up to the north of Ireland for that. Thankfully, it happened naturally for us ... six times.

On the first child, I had a water birth but it was a total disaster. The problem is you have to get the pool into your house a week before your due date and sure the kids from the road were in and out of it 24/7. They were calling to the door with their armbands on begging for a swim. I swear to God I was giving birth and there were sweet wrappers floating on the top of it.

Are You the Perfect Parent or Just Like the Rest of Us?

Your biggest fear as a parent is ...

a.   your child will leave home

b.   your child will never leave home

c.   your child will turn out just like you.

When the kids are going back to school what do you spend the most money on?

a.   school uniform and books

b. a nice pair of pyjamas for yourself to wear at the school gate

c. a huge party you are hosting *because* your kids are going back to school.

What do you put in your child's lunchbox?

a. hummus, quinoa and avocado salad

b. a packet of Oreos and a can of Red Bull

c. nothing – you forget to pack their lunch and have to run back to the school at 11 a.m. with a jam sandwich.

As part of her homework, your daughter is required to make an outfit from recycled materials. Do you?

a. stay up all night making a dress out of toilet rolls with tinfoil earrings to match?

b. cut two holes in a Lidl bag and shove it on her head?

c.   tell her that her uniform belonged to her older sister so 'technically' it *is* recycled materials?

When do you love your kids the most?

a.   when you see them playing happily with your husband in the sunshine.

b.   when you see them playing happily with your husband ... in the rear-view mirror as you drive off for a weekend with the girls.

c.   when they are asleep?

Mostly A: You are the perfect parent and you're probably on Xanax.

Mostly B: You are *deeply flawed* ... like 99.99 per cent of the population.

Mostly C: you need to have Supernanny Jo Frost stay at your house – permanently!

THE LIES WE TELL OUR CHILDREN

☞ That goldfish isn't *dead*, it's just doing the backstroke.

☞ When the ice-cream van plays that music, it means the ice-cream has gone off.

☞ That's just a crease in the photo, I never smoked when I was a teenager.

☞ I *never* fought with my siblings. (We kicked the shite out of each other 24/7).

☞ I didn't start drinking until I was 40. (Actually I was 14).

☞ The tooth fairy only gives 50 cent for top teeth.

☞ Your father was my first and *only* boyfriend. (I slept with half the town.)

☞ The dogs are just giving each other piggy backs … that's all.

☞ You have to be over 18 to become a vegetarian.

☞ There are *no* vegetables in that carrot soup.

☞ The telly only works after 6 p.m.

☞ Your dad and I were just practising our rugby tackles in the bedroom.

☞ You shouldn't have too much screen time – well, that's what is says on Facebook.

Tips for Irish Women Going Abroad

DON'T BOTHER YOUR ARSE WITH A BLOW DRY

Humidity levels are different in hotter countries. Your hair might be as straight as a poker when you board the flight but as soon as your feet touch foreign soil, you will look like you've had electric shock treatment. Don't try to fix it with hair straighteners, instead surrender to the fact that, for the duration of your holiday, you will look like Jon Bon Jovi.

The following are some affirmations you can say to yourself if you accidentally catch a glimpse of your hair in a shop window and start spiralling down into a deep depression:

1. Frizzy can be sexy too.

2. I can handle looking like a member of Whitesnake.

3. I am beautiful ... on the inside.

YOU BETTER BAG IT

Remember to put all your make-up in a plastic bag the night before you go on holidays, otherwise it may be confiscated and you might find yourself wrestling a member of customs to the ground in a bid to retrieve your favourite Benefit mascara. Always use the appropriate bag and not any of the following:

1. a sandwich bag

2. a bin liner

3. a bag from the vegetable section in Supervalu

4. a poo bag.

YOU LOOK LIKE AN OBESE BABY WHALE IN YOUR SWIMSUIT — SO WHAT!

A lot of Irish people are so ashamed of their bodies that they spend all their time on the beach hiding behind windbreakers, rocks and their large children. Some are so desperate to hide their bingo wings and muffin tops that they seek refuge in the deep sea, despite the fact that they can't actually swim. (May they rest in peace.)

DON'T COMPARE AND DESPAIR

When you are abroad you will see a lot of tanned, slim, gorgeous-looking women on the beach playing volleyball. As you watch these women bouncing up and down sexily in their skimpy bikinis, you may find yourself feeling bitter, angry, jealous or even homicidal. We recommend saying the following affirmations to make yourself feel better:

1. I am myself.

2. I am enough.

3. I am going to have another drink. (Because remember: the more you drink, the better you look.)

CONTROL YOUR URGE TO BUY CRAP

Limit your shopping while abroad. You will not be able to fit 300 fake Prada bags, 200 knock-off bottles of Chanel

N°5 and 100 wooden elephant figurines into your Lidl suitcase.

AVOID TAKING SELFIES WHEN DRUNK AND ABROAD

You may think you look rested and beautiful but after a few days in the sun, your head will resemble a scalded tomato, your make-up will continuously slide down your face and your hands will be so bloated that you will barely be able to pick up the phone to take the selfie in the first place. We recommend that all selfies be taken in Dublin airport before going abroad.

FLIRT WHEN ABROAD

Prepare to flirt because there will be very handsome men, with exotic features and very sexy accents (from Manchester and Newcastle).

BOOK YOUR NEXT HOLIDAY WHILE YOU'RE ON HOLIDAY

The good news is there are a lot of cheap deals available if you're willing to accept a few very minor inconveniences

... like the apartment still being under construction when you get there. But who needs a roof when it's 39 degrees at night. Let's face it, you're either pissed or asleep anyway.

Inspirational Quotations from Real Irish Women

You become what you think ... so there's a good chance I'll wake up tomorrow morning looking like a Krispy Kreme doughnut.

SHARON FULLER, DICKSBORO, COUNTY KILKENNY

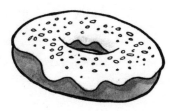

LEARN TO LOVE YOUR MUFFIN TOP

According to health experts, the reason women find it so difficult to lose weight is because diets *do not work*. But, the truth is that the diets are not the problem, *we are*.

Perhaps we take the diets too literally. When Dr Atkins said to eat as much protein as you want he did not mean for us to have eight sausages, six rashers, nine eggs, three steaks, four pork chops and two tins of beans for breakfast.

The 5:2 diet suggests that we fast for two days and eat 'normally' for the other five. This *does not* mean we fast on Monday and Tuesday and eat nothing but Chinese takeaway and Black Forest gateau for the other five.

DON'T BLAME YOUR ARGOS WEIGHING SCALES

For a lot of women, standing on weighing scales can be an extremely traumatic experience. The shock of seeing their weight in numbers can cause them to engage in the following extreme behaviours:

1. Hopping on and off the scales repeatedly in the hope that the numbers will change.

2. Adjusting the dial on the scales.

3. Screaming at the scales when the numbers do not change.

4. Throwing the scales down the stairs.

5. Accusing Argos of selling you 'faulty' weighing scales.

THE THINGS WE SAY TO OURSELVES WHEN THE ZIPPER WON'T GO UP

☞ 'That bloody washing machine shrinks everything.'

☞ 'I'm not going to panic ... it's just water retention.'

☞ 'This jaysus zip is definitely faulty.'

☞ 'This couldn't be a size 14, it must be a 10.'

Case Study 1

Claire Murphy *from Athlone talks about her experience on the Victoria's Secret model diet*

Claire: I am allowed to eat one celery stick, half a cherry tomato and an eighth of a kale leaf a day. It's absolute torture! I feel hungry, irritable and I've no energy. My husband and my children say that I am an absolute nightmare to live with.
Interviewer: How long have you been on this diet?
Claire: Two hours.

Case Study 2

Tracey Savage *from Cabra describes her struggle with dieting*

I just can't stick to any diets because I am a

stress eater. Well, actually, I eat when I'm stressed, relaxed, happy, sad, confused, bored, drunk, sober, tired, lonely, distracted ... and sometimes even when I'm hungry. To be honest, I think I use food ... as an *emotional crutch*.

I also think I'm allergic to certain foods. For example, when I'm having my dinner, I might have a burger, curry chips, a couple of muffins, a chocolate milkshake and a packet of Tayto crisps. Then all of a sudden I would just bloat out ... for no reason. I think I might be a celeriac.

Case Study 3

Louise Lardarse *from Kerry talks about how she believes she can think herself thin*

Louise: I use the power of visualisation to lose weight. I cut images of my favourite celebrities out of magazines and stick them all over the house. Everyday I visualise myself wearing the same bikinis and having the same body as J-Lo and Elle Macpherson.

Interviewer: Are you also sticking to their super strict diet and exercise regime?
Louise: What? No ... do I have to do that as well?

MYTHS ABOUT DIETS

Myth: You won't feel hungry on a diet.
Truth: You will obsess about food constantly ... until you
start hallucinating that your husband's head looks like
a large doughnut and your children look like spare ribs.

Myth: If you don't buy it, you won't eat it.
Truth: You would drive for 800 kilometres at 12 midnight
to get a mint crisp.

Myth: Tracking your food with a diary helps you lose
weight.
Truth: No, it won't, because you'll realise the first 18
pages are just what you had for breakfast.

Myth: If you're tall, you can carry the weight.
Truth: No, you can't. You just look like a tall fat person.

Myth: You will lose weight if you don't eat after 6 p.m.
Truth: Not when you've eaten 20 burgers up until
5 p.m.

THE HELL OF HEALTHY COOKING

There is nothing that will make your *blood boil* more than watching your kids push their food around the plate after you've dragged your arse to an organic food market, peeled eight hundred carrots, blanched five heads of broccoli, roasted 200 new potatoes and slow cooked a corn-fed chicken that you raised yourself.

Experts tell us that if we cook nutritious food daily, we will keep our families healthy. However, recent research has shown that the stress of trying to convince our children to eat it can have serious implications on the health of the *parent*.

The following are some of the physical reactions reported by parents when their children start acting up at the dinner table:

☞ 85 per cent have reported feeling a tightness in their chest, when they see their children flicking carrot batons across the room.

☞ 75 per cent experience shortness of breath when their children start spitting out their peas.

☞ 92 per cent break out into a rash when they see their children gagging at the sight of broccoli.

☞ 80 per cent foam at the mouth when they witness their children shove all the green beans into their napkin.

☞ 65 per cent experience acute rage at the blatant disrespect for cauliflower.

☞ 96 per cent fantasise about leaving the family for good when they see their children picking the onions out of the shepherd's pie.

Case Study

NIAMH DENSE from Blanchardstown talks about healthy eating

I never gave my child baby food from a jar ... because it is full of *adjectives*. In fact, there's adjectives in *everything* you buy in a shop. I always made my own food from scratch. I bought one of those hand blenders from Argos, they're brilliant ... you can do a bag of chips in about three seconds.

COOKING IN BULK IS A LOAD OF BOLLOX

We are often advised to cook in large batches at the beginning of the week but there is nothing that will depress the arse off you more than a menu that looks like this:

Monday: Shepherd's pie

Tuesday: A large bowl of chips with a *tablespoon* of shepherd's pie

Wednesday: An even larger bowl of pasta with a *teaspoon* of shepherd's pie

Thursday: Shepherd's pie sandwiches

Friday: Shepherd's pie soup (with very little shepherd's pie in it).

Do You Have a Fear of the Fitting Room?

If you are trying on a crisp white designer shirt and you accidentally get make-up all over the collar

Do you:

a. Buy it (even though you *don't like it* and it costs €350).

b. Completely panic and start scrubbing it with a baby wipe (then realise they're actually *fake tan* wipes).

c. Shove it back on the rail and then smear make-up on *all* of them, to make it look like it's part of the design.

Which of the following do you find most annoying?

a.   When you admire a red dress in size 12 and ask the sales assistant to try it on, and she hands you a size 20.

b.   When go in to buy a T-shirt and the sales assistant convinces you to buy the jeans, shoes, socks, jacket, scarf, hat, handbag and necklace to go with it.

c.   When the sales assistant tells you she loves the new coat you're trying on and that she bought one herself *for her mother.*

When you enter the fitting room and see yourself from behind

Do you:

a.   Celebrate the fact that you've an arse the size of a small country and start twerking in front of the mirror?

b.   Spiral into a deep depression at the shocking sight of your upper back fat spilling over your discoloured bra strap?

c.   Suck in your tummy as much as you can and when *that* doesn't work tell yourself it's a 'fat mirror'?

When you see another woman trying on the exact same dress as you

Do you:

a.   Feel flattered that such a young attractive woman would choose the same dress as you?

b.   Feel sick because she looks like Gisele Bündchen and you look like Danny DeVito?

c.   Feel homicidal?

Mostly A: You have a mild fear of fitting rooms and should always have a glass of wine before you enter a shop.
Mostly B: You should have a whole bottle.
Mostly C: You have a full-blown, untreatable phobia of fitting rooms and should only ever shop online.

Extract from an Irish Woman's Food Diary

Name: Niamh Foley

Age: 43

Weight: 12 stones 10 pounds (or a bit more)

Name of food plan: The Elle Macpherson Diet

MONDAY **(feeling energised and motivated)**

Breakfast: Low-fat egg white omelette and cup of hot water with lemon. (Elle says that tea is dehydrating ... but this tastes like piss.)

Lunch: Avocado, quinoa and beetroot salad with chicken. (Had to go to six different shops to find the jaysus quinoa.)

Dinner: Steamed fish and steamed vegetables. (Still waiting to feel full and trying to distract myself from the packet of Monster Munch on the sideboard.)

Mood: Starving but *determined* to lose three stone in three weeks and look amazing in that bikini from Marks & Spencer. (If Elle Macpherson can do it, so can I.)

Weight: No change ... *at all.*

TUESDAY **(slight pain in my hole but still determined)**

Breakfast: Three low-fat omelettes (starving from last night) and a large cup of coffee. (Sorry, Elle, but I *can't* do the morning routine with four children under nine without caffeine.)

Mid-morning snack: Two almonds. (Still absolutely bloody ravenous.)

Lunch: Leftover salad with a few dodgy tomatoes. (Didn't have any pomegranate, halloumi, avocados or pumpkin seeds in Lidl.)

Dinner: Grilled low-fat turkey breast with steamed broccoli and courgette. (Added ten dollops of coleslaw for a bit of flavour.)

Mood: Low energy and very irritable so had two bananas ... and a Crunchie.

Weight: Didn't weigh myself but my jeans definitely feel looser.

Note: Actually jeans *are not* looser ... just realised I hadn't closed them.

WEDNESDAY **(lower than a snake's arse)**

Breakfast: Cannot face another jaysus egg white omelette. Had two bowls of Coco Pops instead.

Mid-morning snack: Two almonds ... followed by one Hobnob. (Wondering if Elle even knows what a Hobnob is.)

Lunch: Two mouthfuls of quinoa salad (which I spat out). Nothing else in the house so *forced* to have a cheese sandwich. (I'm sure Elle would understand my dilemma.)

Dinner: Steamed chicken and vegetables (followed by five fish fingers and a fistful of skinny chips left over from the kids' dinner).

9 p.m. snack: Cup of tea with four more Hobnobs. (The guilt was overwhelming ... but not enough to stop me from finishing the packet.)

Weight: Gained one pound.

Mood: Doubting that Elle Macpherson is human at all.

Thursday (losing the will to live)

Breakfast: Skipped breakfast in a bid to counteract the Hobnob disaster.

Lunch: Elle's Super Salad made with kale, spinach, broccoli, celery and a shot of wheatgrass ... followed by a packet of Tayto crisps (low fat).

Dinner: Bowl of butternut squash soup ... followed by two bottles of Pinot Grigio. (Can't be *this* hungry *and* sober at the same time.)

Late-night snack: Six almonds. (What a joke!)

Mood: Disorientated. (Have started hallucinating that my children are little Krispy Kreme doughnuts and my husband is a large Big Mac.)

Weight: Lost one pound. (Actually, no, I didn't. Scales are faulty.)

Friday (rock bottom)

Breakfast: Made an egg white omelette ... and gave it to the dog.

Lunch: A full packet of Pringles.

Dinner: Gave up and went to the all-you-can-eat buffet in the new Chinese restaurant Soon Fatt.

Mood: Do not give a f**k.

Weight: Same as I started.

End of week comment: Good luck, Elle, you're a better woman than I am.

ARE YOU DISCIPLINED WITH FOOD OR ARE YOU JUST A GREEDY HORSE?

When you stop at a petrol station do you buy yourself ...

a. absolutely nothing, because you have incredible control?

b. a bottle of water and a packet of chewing gum to take the edge off?

c. three large Galaxy bars, two packets of Tayto crisps and a Lotto ticket (in the hope that you win enough money to have liposuction)?

You are clearing the table after dinner.

Do you ...

a. throw the leftovers in the bin *immediately* so you won't be tempted to eat them?

b. eat half a meatball from your child's plate then go for a run to burn off the extra calories?

c. shovel the remaining six meatballs and all of the half-eaten cold chips into your mouth before you even reach the dishwasher?

You're at a work party talking to your boss about a possible promotion when suddenly the finger food arrives.

Do you ...

a. wait until the conversation ends and run the risk that there'll be absolutely nothing left?

b. alert your boss to the fact that the food has arrived and offer to get him some?

c. leg it over to the food while he's still talking (trampling over several of your colleagues in the process) and inhale as many chicken wings as is humanly possible?

You are making spaghetti bolognese for the whole family. You want to know if it needs more seasoning.

Do you ...

a. ask your husband to taste it, because you don't want the extra calories?

b. take one *tiny* teaspoon and add the required seasoning?

c. keep tasting it until you've eaten half the pot?

Mostly A: You have incredible self-control but you're probably a *massive* pain in the arse.

Mostly B: You have well-above-par self-control but you're probably a *large* pain in the arse.

Mostly C: You need to get your mouth wired, your stomach stapled and someone to give you an electric shock every time you open the fridge.

Recipes from Ordinary Irish Women

JACINTA'S JUICE DIET

Jacinta Rotund from Kells swears by this special juicy diet on which she loses two stone in two weeks. (Unfortunately, though, she puts it all back on within two days.)

Ingredients
6 spinach leaves
3 kale leaves
half a cucumber
3 apples
2 celery sticks

(Secret ingredient: a couple of Mars bars. You couldn't drink that shite on its own.)

Method

Throw them all in the juicer, have a taste and if it still tastes rotten ... add a Crunchie.

Tip: If this diet is boring the bollox off you by Wednesday, just add a bottle of Malibu.

LINDA'S LUSCIOUS LOW-CAL LASAGNE

Linda Glut from Palmerstown cooks ten trays of this delicious lasagne every week. (Linda lives alone but has a very big appetite.)

Ingredients

155 pasta sheets

20 pounds of mince

20 bottles of tomato ketchup

200 lb block of parmesan cheese (or as Linda calls it, Palmerstown cheese)

100 Easi Singles

Method

It's all about the layering. You do a layer of mince, a layer of pasta, a layer of Easi Singles and a layer of tomato ketchup. You do that 15 times and you top it all off with a shedload of Palmerstown cheese.

Shove the trays in the oven, go out and do a shop and by the time you come back they should be ready.

Tip: For extra crunchiness crumble on seven packets of Tayto crisps.

CAROL'S KILLER COCKTAILS

You'll be carried out unconscious after two of these.

The Cabra Cosmopolitan

Ingredients

an entire bottle of Huzzar vodka

a splash of Red Bull

a load of ice

To garnish:

A mandarin orange rammed on to the glass (easy to peel)

Tip: Get out the karaoke machine ... they'll ALL be singing after one of these

Sex on the Bench

Ingredients

2 bottles of *any* cheap vodka from Lidl

a dash of MiWadi peach

a dash of Lucozade

To garnish:

A few penis straws and some coloured paper parasols stuck into each glass (available at any joke shop)

Warning: Do not try to stand up immediately after having this cocktail

Patricia's Potent Potions Pina Colada

(guaranteed to leave you palatic)

Ingredients

a tin of pineapples from Aldi (it's a bastard trying to chop those pineapples up)

a load of sugar

a large bottle of Bacardi

a massive dollop of coconut cream

ice

To garnish:
A pineapple ring (or any shape you can get ... those pineapples are a b*****d!)

Throw it all into a fruit bowl and mix
Tip: Hide the bowl when your guests arrive so you can drink it ALL yourself.

The Flaming Finglas Cocktail

Ingredients
4 bottles of Southern Comfort (cheapest brand available in Iceland)
6 tablespoons of peppermint schnapps (again, Iceland's your only man)

Pour all the peppermint schnapps into a fluted glass (which just means a tall one). Put a teaspoon over it and pour the Southern Comfort on top of it. It must be layered.

Then light the Southern Comfort with a match (if it doesn't light straightaway, smear some white spirits around the rim of the glass) and watch the blue flames explode.
Warning: Do not let the guests light their own cocktails ... especially if they've had Patricia's Potent Pina Colada.

Coping with the Run-up to Christmas

People look forward to Christmas all year long, only to find themselves sitting with their dysfunctional family on a sofa drinking Tesco's own-brand Irish cream and fighting over whether they will watch *EastEnders* or *Willy Wonka and the Chocolate Factory*.

According to Professor Candid in his new book *Christmas Is a Load of My Bollox*, 82 per cent of parents are stressed out of their bins in the run-up to Christmas.

He outlines some of the things that stress parents out the most:

☞ Discovering that Smyths Toys have run out of the *one* fecking thing their child *really* wants for Christmas.

☞ Hearing the news that the sister-in-law they *hate* is coming over for Christmas dinner.

☞ Spending 18 hours unravelling Christmas lights only to discover that *they don't actually work.*

☞ Having to hoover the sitting room every five minutes because their 'non-shed' tree is shedding all over the place.

☞ Waking up in a cold sweat in the middle of the night having nearly forgotten about Elf on the Shelf.

THE COMA-INDUCING CHRISTMAS CONCERTS

Watching your little darling singing in the school choir is always a pleasure. However, it's the torture of having to sit through two hours of *other* children scratching on violins and murdering 'Silent Night' that will send you over the edge.

The chairperson of the SCCC (Surviving Children's Christmas Concerts) has recommended that parents invest in a product that will get them through the concerts without too much trauma, namely *earplugs.*

THE ORDEAL OF ORDERING ONLINE

A lot of people order online thinking they can avoid the stress of the Christmas shopping only to discover that the 'hassle-free' delivery service is far from hassle-free. The following is a list of stuff that can go wrong:

☞ You take Monday off work and they deliver it on Tuesday.

☞ You spend three hours giving directions to the delivery guy and he's actually standing outside your house.

☞ You are out of the house at the time of delivery and so is your nominated neighbour.

☞ Your nominated neighbour doesn't know they are your nominated neighbour.

☞ The Moulinex Masterchef you ordered has ended up in a sorting office in Balbriggan and you live in Cork.

☞ You drive to collect your Moulinex Masterchef and they refuse to give it to you because you haven't got the correct ID.

☞ You're eagerly waiting for your set of six John Rocha signature wine glasses and they arrive ... in a thousand pieces.

☞ Your Ann Summers parcel has arrived in your nominated neighbour's house and you're too embarrassed to collect it.

THE FUTILE ATTEMPT TO LOSE WEIGHT FOR THE CHRISTMAS

This is probably the *worst* time of year to try and drop the pounds, for the following reasons:

☞ There will be an annual Christmas fair in your children's school and you will *have* to support it by buying 250 chocolate rice crispie cakes, 300 fairy cakes and a large Black Forest gateau that you will eat on the way home.

☞ There will be hundreds of unfinished selection boxes just hanging around the house ... and you hate waste.

☞ You never win anything *ever* but you are guaranteed to win the massive Christmas hamper containing a selection of extremely fattening cheeses, crisps, chocolates and wine which you will happily consume in the space of two days.

☞ Every shop you go into will have a large bowl of Quality Street which you will inevitably *have* to pick from.

Case Study 1

SHEILA McCARTEN *from Cavan talks about her quiet Christmas*

Sheila: Christmas is going to be very quiet for me this year.

Interviewer: Why, are you on your own?

Sheila: No, I have the whole extended family coming over.

Interviewer: Why will it be quiet, then?

Sheila: No one is talking to each other.

Case Study 2

Maura McKenna from Swords talks about getting crap presents for Christmas

Last year, we spent a fortune on Christmas presents for *other* people. We bought my brother and his wife two beautiful cashmere sweaters, which they were delighted with.

Then they handed us *our* Christmas present ... it was card which said, 'Congratulations, you've bought a wheelbarrow for a family in Africa.'

It was a nice idea but we were a bit disappointed ... 'cause we really needed a wheelbarrow ourselves.

THE DIARY OF AN IRISH WOMAN DOING DRY JANUARY

GOALS

☞ Give up alcohol for the entire month.

☞ Look as fabulous as Amanda Holden.

Week One: I feel *fantastic* since giving up alcohol. I am sleeping better, my skin is glowing and I have much more energy. (Mind you ... I'm only off it three hours.)

This is going to be easy for me because I don't drink from Monday to Friday (except sometimes on a Wednesday if I'm having a bad week, or Thursday if I'm off on Friday). I'm actually really excited about this challenge ... who said not drinking has to be boring?

Week Two: Oh sweet Jesus, not drinking is *so* boring. On Wednesday I met up with the girls (who are not doing dry January) at 9.30 p.m. and convinced myself it would be just as much fun without drink. I was *so* wrong. Listening to them talk utter shite, crying into their gin and falling off their bar stools repeatedly almost sent me over the edge. I was back home by 10.15.

Week Three: Last night, I dreamed that I was having a bath in a large glass of Pinot Grigio and my husband said I was shouting 'Hendrick's' in my sleep. (He thought I was having an affair and I had to explain to him that it's actually my favourite gin.)

I read somewhere that we should find other ways to treat ourselves when we are off the booze. So I have been dropping into McDonald's on a regular basis. I will not have a drink before the end of January ... but there is a good chance I might be obese.

Week Four: Went back to WeightWatchers. It's official: I am obese. I've put on two stone and look more bloated than my uncle Tony, who drinks ten pints of Guinness a night followed by ten whiskey chasers.

My skin is *not* glowing (except for the rosacea), I have the energy of a snail and I haven't been included in the latest WhatsApp Group 'Lizzie's Lethal Cocktail Night'. I really need a drink.

Why We Should App-Stain from WhatsApp

The following may explain why WhatsApp makes you want to fire your phone out the fecking window.

☞ The average mobile phone user has approximately 200 WhatsApp groups on their phone but only wants to be in two of them.

☞ 65 per cent said they don't want to be in *any* of them but are too afraid to leave in case they will miss something.

☞ 85 per cent said that the constant pinging sound of WhatsApp notifications sends them over the edge.

☞ 45 per cent hate the fact that they are added to the group without being asked.

Case Study

SANDRA DE BÚRCA from Connemara explains how petrified she is of leaving a WhatsApp group

I woke this morning to find that I was added to 'Big Bernie's Birthday Barbecue'. I don't like Big Bernie and I don't want to go to her fecking barbecue but I can't leave the group because it would look really bad: 'Sandra de Búrca has left the conversation.' Bernie would be so mad I'd probably have to leave the area.

Below is a list of typical WhatsApp groups you might find on an Irish woman's phone.

☞ 4th Class Mammies

☞ 4th Class Mammies (I like)

☞ Siobhan's Hen Party

☞ Siobhan's Naughty Pics from Hen

☞ Siobhan's Wedding Cancelled

☞ Taco Thursday

☞ Prosecco Friday

☞ Slimming World.

Case Study

JEAN MURPHY from Waterford discusses how one WhatsApp group for a child's birthday party almost caused her to have a complete nervous breakdown

It all started when I was added to 'Sophia's Tenth Birthday Party' group. Initially it was just a few harmless messages about who was carpooling to Trampoline World and what time they were leaving.

Then my phone starting hopping off the table with a load of questions about what to get Sophia for her birthday. I could feel my chest tightening.

This was followed by a barrage of messages

about the trouble they had signing the waiver online, which caused me to develop a strange-looking rash and a blinding migraine above my right eye.

Just when I was feeling better, they started discussing who had the Trampoline World socks and whether or not we had to buy them when we got there. The migraine spread to my left eye.

Then came the tsunami of bullshit about who was collecting whose child. This went on for *two fecking days*. Having not slept for 48 hours with a rash that had now spread all over my body and a screaming migraine, I took my child to the party.

At this stage I was kept sane only by the thought that there would be no more jaysus messages and I could leave the group. It was then I heard another ping ... some fucker had started the Thank yous.

My psychiatrist has recommended that I delete my WhatsApp.

WHEN STRESS WRECKS
YOUR FACE

The demands of modern living can be very stressful for women. We are expected to be great at parenting, business, cake-baking, home-making and marathon-running, and all while maintaining the BMI of Elle Macpherson.

Stress can totally and utterly ravage your face and no amount of expensive cream can erase that 'wrecked look' you get from years of this domestic torture.

TIPS FOR MANAGING THE STRESS IN YOUR LIFE

Do not compare yourself to those fake fecking eejits on social media

Try not to be fooled by the photos women post of themselves and their husbands having 'an amazing time' in some exotic location: #feeling blessed #having the best time of our lives #we are all a shower of fake feckers.

Get out of Dodge

If your children are sending you over the edge, go into another room (maybe the bedroom or the closet) where you can find peace and silence – and a bottle of chardonnay you hid there before Christmas.

Stop doing ten million things at the one time

Women can often find themselves cooking an omelette with one hand, mopping the floor with the other, helping their child with her homework while simultaneously giving birth to twins. Remember: just because women *can* multitask does not necessarily mean that we *should*.

Control your crazy horse thoughts

If you have regular thoughts about selling your children on DoneDeal and joining the Buddhist monks on a remote island where nobody is fighting to play Fortnite ... then maybe you need help.

Don't be envious of your friends who *always* seem to be extremely positive and calm. The truth is that they're not Zen ... they're on XANAX.

Case Study

FIONA BEAT from Ennis was feeling extremely stressed and hinted to her husband that she needed a break. On the morning of her birthday, she was elated when said hubby gave her a voucher for a four-star spa hotel

I was so excited, I couldn't believe he had actually understood what I needed. But then he told me something that sent me over the edge. He had also booked himself and the kids into the hotel *and* we were all in the same family room.

Inspirational Quotations from Real Irish Women

Go on that holiday, buy those shoes. Life is too long.

SONDRA. SWORDS

The Torture of Raising a Teenager

Raising teenagers is extremely stressful. The average teenager spends twenty-three hours a day on their phone checking their Instagram, Facebook and Snapchat accounts.

Girls are constantly comparing themselves to photos of their friends on social media with fake boobs, thigh gaps, and lips so inflated they could possibly save their lives in a drowning incident.

Trying to remove a phone from a teenager is as dangerous as removing food from a wild cheetah at feeding time.

HOW TEENAGERS COMMUNICATE

Most teenagers stop communicating with their parents completely and parents are left trying to decode their behaviour in a bid to understand the moody little b******s.

The following is a list of these unusual ways of communicating:

☞ tutting

☞ eye-rolling

☞ grunting

☞ shrugging of shoulders

☞ exhaling loudly

☞ looking anywhere but at their parents

☞ hissing

☞ pulling faces behind their parents' backs.

For most parents, it only seems like yesterday that they were getting kisses from their cute little baby boy and now they're being grunted at by a six-foot giant with acne, a nose ring and a voice like Darth Vader.

THE ANNOYING SHIT THEY DO

☞ Ask for runners that cost 7,000 euro ... per runner.

☞ Wear jeans that are so torn they look like they've been savaged by a pack of extremely angry wolves.

☞ Announce they are gay on a Monday, tell you they're straight on Wednesday, then decide they're pansexual by Friday.

☞ If they're girls, hang around with friends who all have names that end in 'a', such as Eva, Ava, Tara, Sara, Alva, Ciara, Mia, Maya and Mila.

☞ If they're boys, hang around with friends called Luan, Cuan, Juan or Ewan.

☞ Wear so many layers of fake tan that you'd think they're from Morocco, not County Meath.

☞ Play Stormzy's latest album so loudly that people in the *next county* complain.

☞ Describe everything as 'so lit', leaving you thinking they're talking about electricity.

☞ Leave mouldy food in their bedrooms, such as furry apples and a ham sandwich which you vaguely remember packing for their school lunch ... last year.

☞ Think you know *nothing* about drugs ... even though you did that much shit you can't remember a *whole decade.*

STUFF PARENTS DO THAT ANNOY TEENAGERS

☞ being in the same room as them

☞ looking at them

☞ talking to them

☞ existing.

What A Teenager Does Over The Course Of A Typical 12 Hour Da

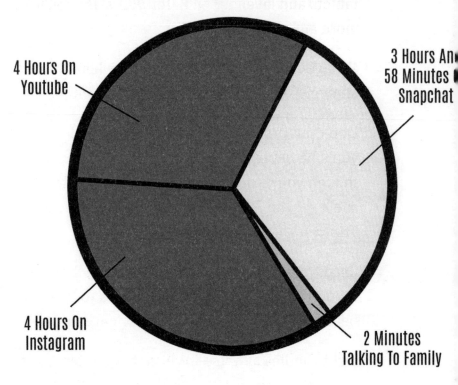

4 Hours On
Youtube

3 Hours An
58 Minutes
Snapchat

4 Hours On
Instagram

2 Minutes
Talking To Family

TIPS FOR PARENTS WITH TEENAGERS DOING THE LEAVING CERTIFICATE

☞ When your teenager starts the exams, go to the health store and buy Rescue Remedy, Kalms tablets and lavender oil ... for *yourself*. (You'll be more anxious then he will.)

☞ Give your teenager loads of space when they are studying – feck off to Spain for six months.

☞ Don't put pressure on your teenager and tell her you'll be happy with whatever she gets (even though you're doing six novenas praying that she'll get the 700+ points and do medicine in Trinity).

☞ Encourage her to follow her passion in life (even though it's killing you that she wants to be a beauty blogger and *not* a neuroscientist).

☞ Light candles at home for luck if you wish ... but not 800 *scented* ones ... or the fumes might kill the dog.

☞ Tell him not to do a post-mortem on his exam. (Someone may mention Q18 and he'll realise he didn't see the questions on the other side of the paper.)

☞ Tell your daughter to stay until the end of the exam (even though she might be finished after five minutes because she can only answer two questions out of 300).

☞ Encourage your teenager to go to bed early (although the chances are that you'll be in a coma before 5 p.m. yourself because you'll have popped *that* many Xanax).

☞ Don't expect to see your son after the Leaving Certificate results come out. (Because *you* will be on the piss for that whole week.)

THE MISSING GENE: WHY THE IRISH ARE SO DIFFERENT TO THE REST OF THE WORLD

Scientists have discovered that some genes which are common among other Europeans are completely missing in Irish people. As a result of recent advances in genetic coding, it is now understood that the Irish DNA is highly unusual and is baffling scientists across the world.

This strange genetic make-up is thought to be the cause of many different dysfunctional behaviours in Irish people.

THE ASSERTIVE GENE

One particular gene that has been identified as missing in the Irish is the assertive gene.

If a group of Irish people are dining in a restaurant and

are not happy with their food, they will complain incessantly to each other but when the manager asks if everything is OK they will look at him, smile and give a resounding 'Yes'.

In fact Irish people are *so terrified* of offending anyone that not only will they *not* complain, they will leave a massive tip.

Another example of this lack of assertiveness is when we get a gift we do not like or already have. Most other nationalities would thank the person and ask for the receipt to exchange it.

But if an Irish person receives a random useless gift (like a foot spa), and even if they've had both of their feet amputated the day before, they will still smile and say, 'That is the nicest gift I have *ever* got in my entire life.'

THE PUNCTUALITY GENE

When Irish people are invited to a social event that starts at 8 p.m. they will usually meet at around 7 for a 'quick' drink beforehand. At 7.58 p.m. they will all look at their watches and unanimously agree that it is time ... to have *another* drink.

They will arrive at the event at 11.30 p.m.

THE ORGANISATIONAL GENE

This gene is vital for the effective running of any country. Scientific research shows that some Irish people do have this gene but unfortunately *not* the people who run the country.

Neuroscientists have found evidence from the brain scans of Irish politicians that they have a complete inability to plan for anything at all. This results in the following:

☞ Running out of water in a three-day heatwave (even though it rains for 362 days of the year).

☞ Traffic coming to a complete standstill when half a snowflake falls from the sky.

☞ A national bread shortage if two snowflakes fall from the sky.

☞ Building 3,000 houses in one small area and providing two car parking spaces.

☞ Providing a public transport system that defies logic where a person may be waiting for seven hours for a bus and then twenty of them come at the same time.

SUE COLLINS & SINEAD CULBERT

The following are some of the genetic mutations that are unique to the Irish population:

THE 'WHITE LIE' GENE

This white lie gene is often activated when an Irish person is asked for their opinion on something. A good example of this is when a friend asks if she looks like she has put on weight. An Irish person will immediately say, 'No, not at all, there isn't a pick on you.'

She will then go further to say, 'Actually you look like you've *lost* weight.' The friend will walk away feeling fantastic and as soon as she's out of earshot, the Irish person will say, 'Jaysus ... she is *obese*.'

Another example of this is when an Irish person is running late for a meeting. They will call their boss and apologise profusely, insisting that they are stuck in traffic on the M50. When the boss asks about the loud noise in the background the Irish person will explain that the noise is just 'torrential rainfall'. The truth is, however, that they are still in the shower.

192

THE CHANCER GENE

Scientists have identified that most Irish people carry this gene but it is only activated in the following groups: property developers, politicians, dentists, solicitors, bankers, pharmacists, electricians, plumbers, estate agents, landlords and every shop owner who charges 20 euro for a bottle of wine that you can buy in France for two euro.

Builders are also notorious chancers. Their original quote of 5,000 euro for a small bit of work on your house can quickly escalate due to 'unforeseen costs' and before you know it you're paying 80,000 euro to build a 1x3 foot extension.

Airbnb is attracting more and more people with the chancer gene. They rent every room in the house including the box room, attic and garden shed. Some even charge 50 euro to rent out the closet under the stairs. Breakfast is not included and it usually costs about 20 euro ... for one sausage.

THE SMALL TALK GENE

This gene is totally unique to Irish people. It blesses us with the talent of being able to talk utter shite to anyone, anywhere, about anything for hours on end.

The topic Irish people love talking about the most is the weather. An Irish person has the ability to say 'It's raining' in eight million different ways:

☞ 'Damp old day, isn't it?'

☞ 'I'd say that rain is down for the day.'

☞ 'That's very wet old rain.'

☞ 'Met Éireann got it wrong again, didn't they?'

☞ 'No sign of that rain clearing up anyway.'

☞ 'Will we ever see the sun?'

☞ 'We won't be getting the barbecue out this weekend.'

☞ 'You wouldn't know what to be wearing.'

THE 'I'M ONLY HAVING THE ONE TONIGHT' GENE

Having this gene can be totally detrimental to an Irish person's health. An Irish person will genuinely tell themselves that they are capable of going out to the pub, meeting their friends and having *one* drink. Unfortunately, when this gene is activated he/she will start saying things like:

☞ 'Ah, another one won't kill me.'

☞ 'Feck it, you only live once.'

☞ 'It's my round anyway.'

Inevitably, this person will end up hammered and twerking on the bar at two in the morning.

THE 'TAKE OFF YOUR SHIRT IF THERE'S ONE RAY OF SUNSHINE' GENE

Unfortunately, a large percentage of the Irish male population are carriers of this gene. A single ray of sunshine immediately causes them to remove their shirts and walk around in gangs, subjecting passers-by to an eyeful of repulsive, pasty, flabby torsos.

Tourists have reported suffering post-traumatic stress disorder after witnessing these shirtless creatures.

THE 'LET'S WAIT AND SEE' GENE

If the fire alarm goes off at work, most nationalities follow health-and-safety procedures and vacate the building immediately. However, Irish people will 'wait and see' if it's a *real* fire and refuse to move until they actually see flames coming out of someone's arse.

Research has shown that the *only* bell they immediately respond to is the one in the pub that the barman uses for last orders.

DOES THE HOUSEWORK HAVE YOU HANGING BY A THREAD?

A recent study shows that women do 60 per cent more housework than men. Professor Anne Weary from the Why Is It Always Left to the Woman Institute believes that the real percentage is more like 99.99 per cent.

Having re-examined the study about the amount of housework women do, she discovered that the women did not answer the questions in the survey properly as they were just too wrecked ... from doing all the housework.

The following table shows the impact housework has on us.

TYPE OF HOUSEWORK	PHYSICAL REACTION	PSYCHOLOGICAL REACTION
Hoovering	Deep sighing	Mild resentment
Emptying the dishwasher	Grinding of the teeth	Low-grade irritation
Dusting	Rolling the eyes	Frustration
Cleaning the skirting boards	Muttering under breath and high blood pressure	Extreme rage
Doing the laundry	Foaming at the mouth	Acute trauma and hallucinations
Cleaning the bathroom	Bouts of nausea	Homicidal tendencies

Amount Of Housework Done By Men And Women

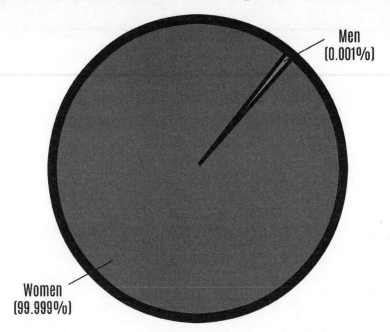

Men
(0.001%)

Women
(99.999%)

MYTHS ABOUT HOUSEWORK

Myth: Cleaning the house leaves you feeling satisfied.

Truth: Yes ... for three and a half seconds, and then the kids mess it up again and you want to jump out a window.

Myth: Cleaning is a good way to burn calories.

Truth: You may burn approximately 250 calories from doing an hour of hoovering but it is so mindnumbingly boring that you will immediately go to the kitchen and consume a whole packet of Hobnobs, which is well over 2,000 calories. In reality, the only way to lose weight from cleaning is to get a cleaning job in the Taj Mahal or hoovering the Vatican.

Myth: You are happier when your house is sparkling clean.

Truth: *You* might be, but your children and husband are tortured because you follow them around with a Dyson all day, polish under their arses and swipe their plates off the table before they've even finished their lasagne.

Myth: Getting the family involved will get the housework done more quickly.

Truth: No, it won't. In the time you've spent begging, bribing and screaming at your kids to fill the dishwasher and explaining to your teenager how to empty the bag in the hoover, you'd have cleaned the whole jaysus house yourself ... twenty times over.

Myth: Getting a cleaner relieves the stress of housework.
Truth: No, it doesn't. You have to tidy the fecking house before the cleaner *even arrives*, and very often when they leave you're 50 euro down and on your hands and knees cleaning it again anyway.

THE FEAR OF BEING JUDGED

All women live in fear of being judged on how clean their house is. We all know the neighbour who calls in for a 'cup of sugar' and then glides her fingers along the mantelpiece to see how much dust is there. You know she doesn't *really* want the sugar because she told you three years ago that she has Type 2 diabetes.

Below are some excuses for *not* inviting people into your house when you haven't cleaned it:

☞ the kitchen is on fire

☞ the microwave has exploded

☞ the dog has rabies

☞ the kids have a highly contagious bug and we are all in quarantine

☞ the house is haunted and we're having an exorcism.

ARE YOU A CLEAN-FREAK OR SICK OF FREAKING CLEANING?

What do you clean your oven with?

a. Cif

b. baking soda

c. deep resentment.

How do you make cleaning your bathroom a pleasant experience?

a. By playing Queen's 'Bohemian Rhapsody' at full volume while you do it.

b. By downing a bottle of cava before you start.

c. By sitting back and watching somebody else do it.

How much time do you spend cleaning your house per day?

a. Four hours. Then a break for twenty minutes. Then four more hours.

b. Under 30 seconds (when you see your mother-in-law's car pulling up outside).

c. None.

What's the first thing you do when you open the door to the laundry room?

a. Enjoy how spacious and clean-smelling it is.

b. Feel mild despair.

c. You can't *actually* open the door to the laundry because you've that much laundry in there.

What's in your fruit bowl?

a. A display of ten different types of succulent, ripe fruits strategically placed to look colourful and inviting.

b. Two rotten bananas, a dodgy-looking apple and a shrivelled pear.

c. Old keys, a broken doorknob, unopened post, a golf ball and four used batteries.

When you look under your bed what do you see?

a. Your own reflection in your extremely well-polished, French-oak, solid-wooden floor.

b. A couple of scattered books on your half-hoovered laminate floor.

c. 35 inches of dust completely covering one pink slipper, two odd socks and a *Hello!* magazine from 2002.

How dirty are your doors?

a. Not dirty at all, any microscopic smudges which appear are eliminated within five seconds.

b. Slightly dirty but nothing a deep clean can't fix.

c. There are actually only a few patches left to indicate it was originally painted 'linen white'.

Mostly A: Marie Kondo needs to watch her back – you deserve your own show.

Mostly B: You need to watch Marie Kondo's show.
Mostly C: You need to go on Marie Kondo's show.

WHEN THE IRISH GO CAMPING

Until recently, camping was never really an option in Ireland due to the 800 years of constant rain. However, as a result of global warming and the special offers on four-man tents in Aldi, there has been an explosion in the numbers of Irish people going camping.

Unlike the Dutch, the French and the Germans, however, Irish people do not a have a *ball's notion* how to behave on a campsite.

The following are some of the embarrassing things they do while camping:

☞ Arrive at the campsite with three cool boxes, four barbecues, eight blow-up mattresses, six camping chairs, two sets of multicoloured festival lights – but without the poles for the tent.

☞ Put up the tent while looking at a YouTube video on 'How to put up the tent'.

☞ Forget that they are staying in a tent made of *polyester* and subject everyone to their conversations at 2 a.m. about 'who is going to take little Rihanna to the toilet'.

☞ Play songs like 'The Irish Rover' by The Dubliners at 800 decibels while drinking 800 cans of Bulmers.

MYTHS ABOUT CAMPING IN IRELAND

Myth: It's a cheap holiday.
Truth: You will spend 500 euro a day on go-karts and slushies, and realise it would have been cheaper to go to Disneyland for three weeks.

Myth: You will get good coverage for your mobile phone.
Truth: You will have to climb a 25-foot sycamore tree and hang out of one of the branches just to get *one bar*.

Myth: Your children will be outside enjoying nature.
Truth: No, they won't. They'll be in the tent killing each other because it hasn't stopped pissing rain the whole time.

Myth: Wi-fi is available on the campsite.

Truth: You will have to roam around for eight hours and lie on the grass in different positions trying to find the wi-fi spots.

Myth: Camping is a relaxing holiday for parents.

Truth: Yes – if you consider setting up a tent for four hours, washing dishes every two hours and packing up for eight hours a relaxing holiday.

Myth: Blow mattresses work.

Truth: You will inevitably wake up at 4 a.m. on the freezing-cold, rock-hard ground and consider pushing your husband off his.

Myth: One token will get you a long, hot shower.

Truth: One token will get you a freezing cold shower for under two minutes, leaving you with no time to rinse out your fecking conditioner.

Myth: Camping is an active holiday which involves cycling, fishing and long hikes.

Truth: The only activity Irish campers engage in is buttering bread for Tayto-crisp sandwiches and walking to reception to get a bottle opener for their Pinot Grigio.

Myth: It's not about *how you look*, it's about reconnecting with nature.

Truth: When you go to the toilets and realise you look like Grizzly Adams, you'll never want to camp again.

PEOPLE WHO USE THEIR MOBILE PHONES ON PUBLIC TRANSPORT

There are many different types of *head wreckers* who use mobile phones while on public transport.

THE LOUDMOUTH

This person is totally unaware that they have a voice that would *wake the dead* and shout so loudly you might be fooled into thinking they are conversing with a friend in Outer Mongolia when, in actual fact, they are talking to someone in Cavan.

After this conversation, everyone in an eighty-mile radius knows this person is being picked up outside O'Hara's pub at two o'clock, they're having bacon, mash and cabbage for dinner and are planning to watch *Fair City*.

Research has shown that sitting beside such a mouthpiece can cause serious damage to the middle ear and even perforate the eardrum.

THE DOZY COW WHO DOES NOT HEAR HER MOBILE PHONE

You may find yourself sitting on a bus feeling relaxed and happy when suddenly a mobile phone starts to ring loudly. Everybody starts to check their *own* mobile phones *except* the person whose mobile phone is *actually* ringing.

Soon everyone figures out where the ringing is coming from, *except* the person who owns the phone. Eventually, the person sitting beside the dozy cow tells her that her phone is ringing.

She picks up her very large handbag and proceeds to rifle through it for what seems like an eternity. Just before she locates the jaysus phone ... the ringing stops. Everyone on the bus sighs with relief. She puts her handbag down ... and the phone starts to ring again. This happens again five more times. This is the longest journey you will *ever* make.

THE PERSON WHO GIVES TOO MUCH INFORMATION OVER THE PHONE

These people have absolutely no shame. If you are unfortunate to be sitting near them you may develop post-traumatic stress disorder after you are subjected to their conversations, which could include anything from a detailed discussion on whether or not they should have their vasectomy, their mother-in-law's IBS symptoms or a blow-by-blow account of the procedure to remove the verruca from their left foot.

If you're *really* unlucky they may even show you the 'before' and 'after' photographs.

THE PERSON WITH THE EMBARRASSING RINGTONE

We have all been on a train or a bus, sitting in peaceful silence, when suddenly a song such as 'Sexual Healing' starts blasting out of another passenger's bag. The passenger, totally mortified, desperately tries to switch their phone off but not before we are subjected to the lyrics 'Wake up, wake up, let's make love tonight. Get up, get up 'cause you do it right'. This person is usually so humiliated they get off six stops before their actual destination.

Other embarrassing songs include:

☞ 'Hello' by Lionel Richie

☞ 'I Just Called to Say I Love You' by Stevie Wonder

☞ 'Call Me' by Blondie

☞ 'You Raise Me Up' by Westlife

☞ 'Total Eclipse of the Heart' by Bonnie Tyler

☞ 'Hello' by Adele

THE PERSON WHO BURSTS OUT LAUGHING SPORADICALLY AT SOMETHING THEY ARE WATCHING ON THEIR MOBILE PHONE

You are sleeping on the train on a three-hour journey to Galway when you are suddenly woken by the person beside you who is laughing hysterically at something on his mobile phone.

You settle yourself back to sleep only to be woken again by this person doubled over laughing. You lean across to see what is so hilarious only to discover that he is looking at a cat coming down a slide backwards wearing welly boots and sunglasses. And after this video, he starts watching Liverpool v Man United ... now you know you're fecked.

THE PERSON WHO SPEAKS IN CODE

This person usually speaks in a low voice and thinks she is speaking in code but everyone on the bus knows *exactly* what she is talking about.

She has a conversation about 'an amazing dinner' she had for the 'first time' with her boyfriend the night before. She didn't plan to have 'dinner' with him because they only just met but 'one thing led to another' and suddenly they were having 'dinner' on his bathroom floor.

She describes how the 'dinner' was 'hot', but unfortunately the 'dinner' only lasted two and a half minutes.

Inspirational Quotations from Real Irish Women

Twenty years from now, it's the things you *didn't* do that you'll regret, not the things you *did* ... except snogging your boss at the office Christmas party – in front of his wife.

Becky, Coolock, Dublin 5

WHEN A HOLIDAY AWAY WITH THE GIRLS IS BETTER THAN THERAPY

It is *so* important for a woman's well-being (and her family's) to schedule in a few short breaks with her close friends throughout the year. Dr Spent from the Give Me A Jaysus Break Institute warns that if women wait *too* long to take a break, they may go on a holiday and never come back.

EXCUSES WOMEN GIVE TO THEIR PARTNERS TO GET AWAY FOR A GIRLS' WEEKEND

☞ I'm going away to get some rest and relaxation. (You won't get a wink of sleep 'cause you'll be drinking the head off yourself for three days straight.)

☞ It's my friend's fortieth birthday. (She actually turned 43 last year.)

☞ I just want to catch up with my sisters (even though you speak to them every day for *at least* an hour).

☞ I'm taking my mother to Italy because she has never seen Rome. (She goes every year to see the pope.)

☞ The flight to Lisbon was practically free. (It cost you 350 euro.)

☞ I thought you might want to spend some quality time with the kids.

☞ My good friend had a baby in Canada and I *have* to go and see her. (She's not a close friend at all and you're just using it as an excuse to see Niagara Falls.)

☞ Myself and the girls are going on a spa weekend to cleanse and detox. (You'll probably need a liver transplant from all the wine you'll consume in between hot-stone massages.)

THINGS YOU ARE NOT ALLOWED TO DO ON A GIRLS' WEEKEND

1. Talk about your kids, your husband or your dog.

2. Show photos of your kids, your husband or your dog.

3. Phone your kids, your husband or your dog.

THINGS YOU END UP DOING (AFTER TEN GIN AND TONICS) ON A GIRLS' WEEKEND

1. Talking about your kids, your husband and your dog.

2. Showing photos of your kids, your husband and your dog.

3. Phoning your kids, your husband and your dog.

TIPS FOR GOING ON HOLIDAY WITH THE GIRLS

☞ Get extensions on absolutely everything: Your nails, your lashes, your hair – and your bank overdraft.

☞ Tell your husband your flight is at 9 a.m. when it's actually at 9 p.m. (This way you get a whole day to yourself at the airport.)

☞ Pop into Lidl and buy 15 mini bottles of wine to stick into your handbag in case Ryanair runs out of alcohol.

☞ Go into duty free and spray yourself with 250 designer perfumes (even though you've no intentions of buying any of them because you've packed a bottle of Impulse).

ESSENTIALS TO PACK FOR A GIRLS' HOLIDAY

☞ Six pairs of shorts, six sun dresses, seven bikinis, five dresses for evening wear, three pairs of white linen trousers, fifteen pairs of sandals (even though you'll wear the same jaysus pair of black shorts and pink T-shirt you got from Penneys for the entire holiday).

☞ An extra suitcase to bring home the 25 fake Dolce & Gabbana handbags, 15 pairs of fake Ray-Bans (Roy-Bans), 200 packets of ibuprofen, six months' supply of antibiotics and 50 Diflucan (all for under 20 euro).

☞ Factor 50 sunscreen (which you will *never* take out of your bag).

☞ Aftersun lotion (which you will *have* to use because you didn't take the factor 50 out of your bag).

QUESTIONS YOU ARE NOT ALLOWED TO ASK WHILE ON HOLIDAY

1. How do you think Brexit will affect Irish business?

2. Do you think Trump will be re-elected?

3. How's work going?

QUESTIONS YOU ARE ALLOWED ASK WHILE ON HOLIDAYS

1. Can I have another jug of sangria?

2. Will someone help me up? I've just drunk a whole jug of sangria.

3. Do you think our waiter, Jose, is married?

4.   Do you think Jose would *like* to be married and live in Ireland?

5.   Do you think my 6x6 foot Oriental handwoven rug will fit into the overhead bin?

Are You a BFF (Best Friend Forever) or a TFT (Total Fecking Traitor)?

On the day of her wedding your friend walks out of the hairdresser looking like the love child of Jon Bon Jovi and Bonnie Tyler.

Do you:

a. Tell her she shouldn't have gone to a hairdresser called Singe & Curl, quickly smuggle her into the boot of your car and bring her to *your* hairdresser?

b. Tell her it's gorgeous and post thousands of pictures of her mullet from every angle on Instagram and Facebook?

Your friend comes back from a six-month trip around the world and has obviously enjoyed the local cuisines a bit *too* much.

Do you:

a.   Try not to focus on the fact that she is now morbidly obese and compliment her tan?

b.   Ask her if she had to book two seats on the flight home?

Your friend's ex-boyfriend (who you've always secretly fancied) asks you out.

Do you:

a.   Decline and eat five boxes of Krispy Kreme Doughnuts while imagining sticking pins into a voodoo doll of your friend?

b.   Go out with him, move in with him and marry him ... all in the space of twenty-four hours?

Your friend tells you her *juiciest* secret and makes you swear you won't tell anyone.

Do you:

a.   Refuse to divulge *even* if you are being dangled over the edge of a cliff with a gun pointed at your head?

b.   Only tell a *few* people ... like your sister, your mother, your cousin, your personal trainer, the postman and everyone you meet on the street?

Your friend shows you pictures of her new boyfriend who she thinks looks like Hugh Jackman.

Do you:

a.   Tell her you think he's gorgeous even though you think he looks less like Hugh Jackman and more like a Hobbit?

b.   Make an appointment for her at Specsavers?

You're on a night out. your friend has done too many shots of tequila and has passed out at the table.

Do you:

a.   Take her home and put her to bed?

b.   Quickly move to another table, slip on some shades, put on a foreign accent and pretend you've never seen her before in your life?

Mostly A: Congratulations you are the perfect BFF.
Mostly B: You are probably a perfect contestant for *Love Island*.

TIPS FOR VALENTINE'S DAY

☞ Don't get jealous when you see your neighbour getting 800 roses delivered to her house. The chances are she sent them to herself.

☞ Walk around the place completely naked. This will definitely turn your partner on ... although the other people in the restaurant might complain.

☞ When your wife tells you she doesn't want anything for Valentine's Day what she *really* means is to book her favourite restaurant, buy her expensive jewellery, hire a plane and skywrite the words 'I love you' for the whole world to see.

☞ If you're singing Whitney Houston's 'I Will Always Love You' on their voicemail and texting love poems every five minutes, your Valentine is less likely to take *you* out and more likely to take a barring order out.

☞ If you're alone on Valentine's Day, try to look at the positives. You might have to buy your own box of Milk Tray, but you don't have to share them.

☞ Book the babysitter early. You don't want to cancel your table for two and have to ask for a table for four.

	YOUR FIRST VALENTINE'S DATE	TWENTY YEARS LATER
Where you went	A posh new restaurant in town	The Chinese restaurant around the corner
What you wore	Sexy lingerie, a tight red dress and ten-inch heels	Whatever you had on you that morning
What you got	A huge cuddly toy, a box of chocolates, a bunch of flowers and two tickets to Paris for the weekend	A scratchcard

Case Study 1

LOUISE Low from An Naul talks about how her husband surprises her on Valentine's Day

My fella is great at surprises. I'd be sitting watching the telly and the door would fly open and he'd say, 'Louise, we're going out for dinner ... to IKEA.'

Case Study 2

DERVLA PHONY from Foxrock talks about the amazing gifts she gets from her husband on Valentine's Day

He is sooo romantic. Every Valentine's Day, he showers me with gifts. We are sooo close, such a team ... he lives in Dubai for 362 days of the year, but we're always on FaceTime.

Irish Women's Biggest Fears

The next WeightWatchers meeting

Because you're just back from holidays and you consumed 200,000 calories ... a day.

Looking at yourself in the mirror after a night out

Because 18 gin and tonics and 20 shots of tequila gives you the complexion of a baboon's arse.

The gym

Because you know that when you're on the treadmill you look like a hippo having a seizure.

The monthly phone bill

Because no matter what 'unlimited package' you get, your bill is always astronomical from hours of talking shite to your friends.

A surprise visit from 'the in-laws'

Because you'd rather do a bungee jump off the Spire than see the look of judgement on your mother-in-law's face when she sees the state of your kitchen.

Running out of petrol on the M50

Because you tell yourself you've enough petrol to get you home even though the red light on the dashboard has been flashing for the last two hours.

Control pants

Because, deep down, we know they just push the fat somewhere else.

Wearing a bikini when you're abroad

Because your skin is so blue that when you lie on an Italian beach, they start poking you with sticks because they think you're dead.

Not wearing the right bra when you're running the marathon

Because the last thing you want is to be seen 'bouncing' towards the finishing line ... on the Nine O'Clock News.

Extract from An Irish Woman's Wellness Diary

THIS WEEK'S THEME: PATIENCE

This week, I will try to be more patient. I will remain calm, centred and have compassion for all living things. (Although if the neighbour's dog doesn't stop f***ing barking I will get a rifle and shoot it in the head.)

Monday 10/6/19 (A night from hell)
I was woken up at 3 a.m. by my son, who was convinced there were ghosts in his room. I remained patient with him (and with my husband, who *never, ever* wakes up when the kids need us) and showed him that it wasn't ghosts ... just

the shadows from the trees outside (although it did look like something from *Stranger Things*).

He woke up again screaming and, again, I didn't react (nor did my husband, because he was *still* in a coma, the lazy fecker). I brought our son into our bed, where he tossed, turned and whacked me in the face repeatedly with his little arm (which is when my husband started snoring).

At 4 a.m., I went into my son's room to try and get some sleep but got completely freaked by *that* shadow. (Shouldn't have watched those six episodes of *Stranger Things*.) I eventually fell asleep with a baseball bat in my arms.

I woke up at 7 a.m., fell out of the bunk bed, nearly broke my neck, stumbled downstairs and *still* managed to remain patient ... until my husband announced that he'd had one of the best night's sleep *ever*. That's when I lost my shit and fired a box of Rice Krispies at his head.

Will try harder tomorrow.

TUESDAY **(Rage at the roundabout)**
I was listening to my Deepak Chopra mindfulness CD on my way back from collecting the kids from school when a car cut in front of me. Although I wanted to ram into the back of him and send his new Mercedes flying into the ditch – I

didn't. I remained calm and in control (while giving him the finger).

I caught up with him at the next set of traffic lights and he cut across me again. This time, all the deep breathing in the world could not contain my rage as I put the foot down and followed the f***er to the next set of traffic lights.

I pulled up beside him, rolled down my window and used that many expletives that even Gordon Ramsay would have been red-faced. It was then that my son pointed out that the driver was in fact ... the new principal of the school.

Deepak would *not* be proud.

WEDNESDAY (Waiting impatiently)

I arrived at my dental appointment and sat down to read *The Power of Now* by Eckhart Tolle. Forty-five minutes later (having read the chapter on being non-reactive), I approached the secretary and enquired about the delay. You'd swear I had asked her to saw off both her legs and eat them. (Even Tolle would have struggled not to react to *that* face.)

After another thirty-five minutes (having read ten magazines on root canal), I approached the desk again, desperately trying to remain patient. At this point, she told me that Dr Nulty was a *very* busy man, an *extremely* sought-after dentist and that I was *very* lucky to have an appointment with him.

No longer able to remain non-reactive, I told her that *I* was a very busy woman and *she* was extremely lucky that I didn't slap her around the head with the teeth-whitening leaflets. I also reminded her that she was a secretary to a dentist, not f***ing Bono.

I was very proud of the way I did not react to the security guard as he escorted me out of the building.

THURSDAY **(Help me, Oprah)**

I started the day by watching an Oprah Winfrey masterclass on 'How To Be Patient', which was interrupted by a text from Eir to say my latest bill was €864.20. Three hours and 25 automated messages later, I finally got through to a trainee and tried to explain that I had been overcharged.

I *really, really* tried to follow Oprah's advice but the trainee hadn't a fecking clue what she was doing. Suffice to say, I'm now with Vodafone.

Friday (The last straw)

The day started off well. I had newfound levels of patience.
Was tolerant to the kids, husband, work colleagues ...
Even managed not to react to the dog barking – for the first
15 mins ...
May Rover rest in peace.

THE ORIGIN OF WELLNESS

Inspirational Quotations from Real Irish Women

As my mother always said, *'Je ne regrette rien* ... I don't remember anything.'

MARY DOYLE, TERMONFECKIN, COUNTY LOUTH

WHAT NOT TO GET YOUR MOTHER FOR MOTHER'S DAY

A large study carried by the NAJYCI (Not Another Jaysus Yankee Candle Institute) looked at what women *really* want for Mother's Day. Thousands were interviewed, and the findings revealed that 99 per cent received crap they just *did not* want.

The following is a list of some of the shite they received:

☞ dodgy flowers from a petrol station

☞ a small frying pan from Home Store + More

☞ an ornament duck playing a violin

☞ a body lotion from Aldi

☞ a face cloth

☞ a dying plant from Lidl

☞ a cheap face mask (that burns all your skin off)

☞ an oil room diffuser that smells like leather, sour milk and a splash of urine

☞ another jaysus cookbook.

Case Study 1

CIARA BYRNE *from Carlow explains how she gives her husband specific instructions about what she wants for Mother's Day*

I don't want expensive gifts. I just tell him to go into Lidl and the first thing he'll see are the lovely bunches of flowers in front of him. I tell him to walk *right past* the flowers and go down the second aisle where all the lovely boxes of chocolates are ... *ignore them* and go straight down to the alcohol section where he can get me two large bottles of gin.

Case Study 2

Siobhan O'Connell from Roscommon describes her Mother's Day last year

I had just taken up running and had hinted that I wanted something fitness-related. I thought they might get me a new pair of Nike runners or perhaps a Fitbit but instead they got me a book ... *Run Fat Bitch Run.*

Case Study 3

One woman who wished to remain anonymous (to protect the feelings of her husband and children) describes the repeated disappointments she has had on Mother's Day

I don't want my family to think I am ungrateful, but if I get another set of oven gloves or an apron with 'World's Greatest Mother' on the front I will seriously go over the edge.

Case Study 4

MARIE DEVLIN from Drogheda knows the best gift to give any mother on Mother's Day

Interviewer: So what *do* women want?
Marie: Women don't want very expensive presents for Mother's Day. The thing we want doesn't cost much at all, in fact it's completely free.
Interviewer: Quality time with your family?
Marie: No, five fecking minutes to ourselves.

SELF-HELP LANGUAGE WE USE TODAY VERSUS WHAT WE SAID 20 YEARS AGO

TODAY	20 YEARS AGO
Feel the fear and do it anyway	Ah, will ya just get on with it
You can heal your life	You'll be grand
Stop the negative self-talk	Stop talking shite

I am beautiful	There's nothing wrong with me
I trust in the universe	Please, sweet Jesus …
It's all happening perfectly	It's all falling to shit
I can handle it	Leave it with me
Focus on internal joy	Stop your whinging
Wake up to the abundance	You're a spoilt bollox
Focus on the process instead of the outcome	Will ya look at what you're doing
You can handle it	Give yourself a shake

The law of attraction is operating	You brought that on yourself
I am in control	I am f***ed
Visualise your goals	What's for you won't pass you
Gratitude is the attitude	Thanks be to f**k for that
The power is within you	Get off your lazy arse
I am enough	You think you're great
I love myself	I have a smell of myself

INSPIRATIONAL QUOTATIONS FROM REAL IRISH WOMEN

Money is the root of all evil but a certain amount of it is good for the nerves.

CAROL BROKE, EFFIN, COUNTY LIMERICK

CAN YOU MANAGE YOUR MOOLA?

1. Do you make a list *before* you go grocery shopping so you stick within your €85 budget . . . and then spend €50 in Krispy Kreme Doughnuts on the way home?

2. Have you changed from Electric Ireland, to Airtricity, then to Energia, then back to Electric Ireland only to discover that you've *only* saved a total of €2.50?

3. Are final reminders a normal part of your life?

4. Do you drive around to ten different supermarkets to get the 'best deals' saving yourself €10 only to realize you've spent €50 on petrol?

5. When you use your debit card in shops do you frequently hear the words 'That doesn't seem to have gone through, do you want me to try again?'

6. Does the sight of a postman walking towards your door holding envelopes trigger a massive panic attack?

7. Do you see the words 'insufficient funds' every time you try and get cash from an ATM?

8. Do you put your heating on full blast and forget to close the windows?

9. Do you *refuse to* put the heating on and walk around your house wearing 25 coats?

10. When it comes to buying a round of drinks for your friends, do you *hide in the toilets* so they think you've gone home and then go back out once *someone else* has bought a round?

Mostly No: You're probably completing this questionnaire while on a yacht with Richard Branson

Mostly Yes: You are probably answering this questionnaire by candlelight because your electricity has been cut off.

A Survivor's Guide to Getting an Extension

A recent server has shown that getting an extension to your house is extremely stressful and can cause people to lose the following:

☞ all their money

☞ all their hair

☞ all their hope.

95 per cent of survey participants reported that since they finished their extension, they *cannot* do the following:

☞ Look their architect in the eye ('cause he spent all their money).

☞ Watch *Grand Designs* ('cause it *never* works out that way).

☞ Walk past TileStyle without slipping into depression.

☞ Look out the small Velux window (because they should have gone for a bigger one).

☞ Go into a kitchen showroom without crying.

☞ Let the kids into the extension because if they ruin the newly painted walls they'll be f***ing killed.

☞ Check their current account (because they have 00.03 cent left in there).

SOME TIPS TO HELP YOU SURVIVE THE TRAUMA OF GETTING AN EXTENSION

☞ If the builder gives you a quote of 35,000 euro, always have a contingency plan (of *another* 35,000 euro).

☞ Visualise your perfect extension – then let that vision go because it won't look *anything* like it after all the fecking compromises you will have to make.

☞ If the builder tells you they will start in June and finish in September, you can assume it won't finish until December – of the following year.

☞ Don't be talked into things you don't want, you'll be staring at those animal print porcelain bathroom tiles for the next ten years.

☞ The architect might think ten extra skylights will give your bedroom the *wow* factor, but you'll have to spend 5,000 euro on new blinds or you will *never* sleep again.

☞ Take time to make big decisions. You may have thought those oversized LED downlights would look great in your kitchen, but now every time you switch them on it feels like a scene from *Close Encounters of the Third Kind.*

☞ Try not to react to your neighbours who claim that your extension is taking away 'all of their

light'. The f***ers never, ever open their curtains anyway.

BE PREPARED FOR THE BITCHY COMMENTS FROM COMPETITIVE NEIGHBOURS WHEN THEY SEE YOUR NEW EXTENSION:

☞ 'Those tiles are *amazing* ... very difficult to keep clean, though.'

☞ 'It's very *different*, isn't it?'

☞ 'I see you went for the *smaller* skylights.'

☞ 'You went for the French doors instead of the sliding doors ... well, they *are* cheaper.'

☞ 'The wood effect is *nearly* as good as real wood.'

When the build is over, don't fool yourself into thinking that you will never do this again. You'll forget the trauma, the pain and you *will* do it again – just like childbirth.

How To Get Rid of Cold Callers from Your Door

Recent research has found that 5 p.m. can be one of *the most stressful* times of the day for a lot of women because of having to answer the door to annoying cold callers.

At this time of the day, the average woman might find herself peeling carrots, googling the Irish word for 'scarf' for her daughter's homework while screaming at her twelve-year-old son to stop playing Fortnite.

If the doorbell rings during this time, an unusually high amount of cortisol is released into the woman's bloodstream causing very high levels of frustration, extreme aggression and, in some cases, psychotic episodes.

WHAT TO DO WHEN THE GUY FROM AIRTRICITY CALLS

The sight of a person wearing a blue high-vis vest and carrying a clipboard can often trigger feelings of rage and despair.

The following are some guidelines on how to deal with the man from Airtricity without physically or verbally abusing him:

☞ Put on a fake Brazilian accent and pretend you are a nineteen-year-old au pair with no English (even though you're a forty-something woman from Monaghan with a mop of curly red hair).

☞ Open the sitting-room window and tell the man from Airtricity that you cannot open the door because your dog is a vicious Rottweiler who has already attacked the guy from Energia. (Your dog is *actually* a fourteen-year-old chihuahua with no teeth and on heart medication.)

WHAT TO DO WHEN POLITICAL CAMPAIGNERS CALL

☞ Pretend you are a candidate yourself and bore the arse off them with *your own* agenda.

☞ Wreck their heads by repeatedly asking the question, 'What are you going to do about the dog poo problem in the area?'

☞ Send your six-year-old to answer the door and pretend you're not home (and hope they don't call social services).

HOW TO AVOID GIVING YOUR BANK DETAILS TO THE RABBIT REHABILITATION CENTRE IN ROSCOMMON

☞ If you are an animal lover, avoid answering the door completely, otherwise you will end up sponsoring three hundred injured rabbits, going into mortgage arrears and spending all your time reading updates on how Ruby the Rabbit's recovery from her ear operation is going.

WHAT TO DO WHEN RELIGIOUS ORDERS CALL

☞ Tell them you would love to go to their religious meeting but, unfortunately, it clashes with your weekly black mass and human sacrifice ceremony.

☞ Ask them what God is going to do about the dog poo problem in the area.

WHAT TO DO WHEN THE TV LICENCE INSPECTOR CALLS

☞ Hide in the kitchen and do not answer the door. If he looks in the kitchen window, throw yourself onto the ground, roll across the kitchen floor and crawl out into the hall. If he looks through the letterbox and shouts, 'I can see you', simply roll onto your back and pretend to be dead.

☞ If you are a very brave individual, answer the door and brazenly tell the inspector that the reason you have not paid for your licence is because you do not own a television, even though you have a 50-inch TV in every room. (If he hears your children fighting over the remote control in the background, just smile sweetly and tell him you'll pay online.)

Do You Have the Self-Esteem of a Snail?

You are wearing your swimsuit on the beach

Do you:

a.   Take pictures of your arse and post them on Instagram every five minutes?

b.   Hide behind rocks or your very large children?

c.   Jump into the sea and stay there for hours even though you can't really swim?

You're going down an escalator in a shopping centre and you see yourself in a large mirror.

Do you:

a.   Take a picture of your own reflection and post it on Instagram?

b.   Leave the shopping centre and go straight to the gym?

c.   Feel sorry for the wrecked, ancient-looking woman in the mirror ... *not* realising it's actually *you*?

Which do you find most terrifying?

a.   Giving a public presentation.

b.   Jumping out of a helicopter from 10,000 feet.

c.   Sitting in a hairdressers for over three hours and having to stare into a mirror.

How long do you look in the mirror?

a.   As long as it takes to make me look fabulous (and that's not long).

b.   Not very long because I put my make up on while I'm driving.

c.   Long enough to see the huge pores, deep wrinkles, crow's feet, sagging skin, black bags ... do I need to go on?

Mostly A: You either look like Charlize Theron or you're totally delusional.
Mostly B: Your self-esteem is lower than a snake's arse.
Mostly C: You really need to love and accept yourself as you are (or find a really great surgeon).

Inspirational Quotations from Real Irish Women

It's not *how much* you spend on your clothes, it's *the way you wear them*. I have a jacket that cost 10 euro but when I'm wearing it ... it looks like it cost 15 euro.

Sinead Hanlon, Horetown, Wexford

Acknowledgements

We would like to thank our editor Ciara Considine, who came up with the idea to write this book. Thank you to Michelle Culbert for her feedback and Margaret Culbert for her support. Thanks for Ciara Kenny for her brilliant illustrations.

Finally, a big thanks to our husbands, Rogier Meijer and Phelim Drew, for looking after the kids (Sophia, Leon, Vivian, Milo, Lily and Seanie) while we wrote the book.